The Dressing Table

By Mary Lorine Buckman

with Louise Harris

This book is dedicated to the many people who have made me whom I am today. My husband, Bob, is everything to me and my best friend. Erik, Todd and Seth, my children, have supported me with this project. My grandson, Demetrius, is a joy in my life. My siblings, Rebecca and Roger, are there for me whenever I ask. Dr. Andrew Saqua encouraged me to write this book. My biological aunt Ruth has helped me after my mother died. My best female friend, Sally, who is always there supporting me. My cousin, Shannon, who did a DNA test that helped me find my biological family. I wouldn't have written this book without God's influence throughout my life and each of their inputs.

ACKNOWLEDGMENTS

This book moved from idea to finished product with the help of many people. Bob, my husband, took pictures, dealt with technological issues, supported me, talked with me about the project and encouraged me throughout the process. I love him so much. My best friend, Sally, has offered me the shoulder I needed when it became necessary. She always set aside time for me and provided information for the book. Her sister Nancie shared her miracle with me for the conclusion of the book. Rebecca, my sister, shared her stories and encouraged me during the project. Erik, Todd and Seth, my children, who provided stories and helped with technological issues. My adoptive parents, Richard and Peggy Davis, raised me the best way they knew, especially my mother who created the person I am today. Mom encouraged me to go to cooking school and watched Erik for many years when I was a single mother. My biological parents gave me life and had the courage to put me up for adoption to two great people. Two special friends from high school, A.S. and A.P., who inspire me daily even though I haven't heard from them in many years. Their inspiration is found in the desire to get this project finished. Dr. Bennett who took care of my sons and me when it was necessary. Jeannette Turner who pointed me to Louise Harris.

I want to especially thank Louise of LAST Research and Editing, www.lastresearchandediting.com, who compiled the stories, directed me on what to do, edited the book, helped me along the way, introduced me to Ellie D'Sa and managed the project. She also marketed the book. Thank you to Ellie of D'Sa Designs, www.dsadesigns.com, who designed the cover of the book.

I wanted to make one last note. Because my mother went to nursing school, I have been thinking about the doctors, nurses, first responders, postal clerks, supermarket clerks and others who have worked to keep all of us safe from the coronavirus disease afflicting the world as I wrote this book. They have done an amazing job in a difficult situation. Without their help, I might not be here to finish my cookbook. They also inspired me to write a special section of recipes. Thank you.

CONTENTS

FOREWORD

It takes hard work to become an accomplished chef. Besides learning the trade, chefs, like other business professionals and artists, must have mentors. These are the people who inspire us and help us become the people we are today. For me, my mentor is Peter Kreuziger, who owns the restaurant where I worked. He truly represents what God tells us to do: "Do unto others as you would do for me." He has helped me throughout my career as a chef but also as a human being. He often gave me money when I needed to pay bills. He would not fire me when I was late because of an issue with my children. He did so much for me. My cookbook had to include his story. His story will show his accomplishments. Mentors, including mine, will inspire others to be the best they can be. As you read his story, you will learn why Kreuziger inspires me and how that inspiration led me to where I am and how I cook today. Even though I don't work for him anymore, he still helps me and inspires me. I want you to be inspired too. Read about his life.

Peter Kreuziger began his career when he was 16 and living in Austria. He decided on the hotel industry because he wanted to see the world. He knew that the hotel industry would allow him to see the world, so he qhose those courses when he went to university. The program in Austria required participants to study one year in Spain, one year in Italy, one year in England and one year in France. Therefore, the students would learn five languages before they are done. Kreuziger chose to learn English in America. Once he was here, he never went back to Austria. He finished his university studies in New York. Before attending Cornell University for hotel management, Kreuziger started working as a waiter at a German-speaking restaurant in New York City. The restaurant that could seat 1,000 people and took up a whole city block was known as Luchowz at that time. It was there that he learned English while serving German customers. He was immersed in German food and culture while serving and living in New York. He got to know the regular customers when he worked at the restaurant for three years. Some of the regulars suggested he continue his schooling at Cornell, which was and still is a premier university for hotel management. In 1967, he attended Cornell.

At Cornell, he became manager of the Faculty Club where he improved his hospitality skills and learned from others. He arranged a boat party for a professor. This party introduced him to powerful people in the hotel industry. These hotels were under German-speaking leadership and their English wasn't very good, so they relied on Kreuziger who knew both German and English languages. He continued to work at the restaurant and told the members to form a union. He joined and became a dues-paying member. He continued working at the restaurant through college. When he graduated, he interviewed with 26 companies who saw the value in having Kreuziger on the team. He was offered 25 positions. The one that didn't offer him a position was a company that provided information on business practices around the world. In the form rejection letter, the letter-writer misspelled European. "I circled the word and sent the letter back to the company," Kreuziger said.

He moved to Jacksonville, Fla., to work for a development company. This business built country clubs, restaurants and hotels throughout the United States and at key resorts in the world. He built 600 hotels in Bermuda, 12 restaurants and many more in other places while working for this development company. He hired a chef for the Hotel Royal Orleans without ever meeting him. The chef was recommended by others that Kreuziger knows. Therefore, he decided he would be a good fit. The chef turned out to be the right person for the job, making the restaurant in the hotel successful and well-known. During this time, he fell in love. Even now, his wife is a part of everything he does.

In 1975, Kreuziger wanted to do something different. He decided to partner with the chef from the Hotel Royal Orleans. He got a loan and wanted to buy a property. He came across this restaurant in Dunedin, Fla., that was falling apart and dirty. The downtown area of Dunedin had empty storefronts in 1975 and no restaurants were there. He and the chef bought the place and renovated it into Bon Appetit. Kreuziger opened his own company in 1976 managing hotels and restaurants. He started the Dunedin Merchants Association and was a main part of the revitalization of the town. Today, the restaurant was voted in the top 100 views in the country. Wherever you sit in the restaurant, you can see the water. Kreuzier owns Hillsborough Park Cafe, Weddings on Sand Key, Romantic Honeymoon Island and other destinations or restaurants. He travels to and from Austria regularly and is still working in his 70s. He is happy.

Due to circumstances, I had to leave Bon Appetite, but the restaurant, the people and Mr. K still hold special places in my heart.

INTRODUCTION

Dressing table has many meanings, which is why I chose it as the perfect title. Let's begin with dressing.

Dressing is used on salads. It also refers to how a table is presented. Chefs worry about presentations as much as the taste of the food, but the presentation doesn't stop with the food. The table must be dressed or presented in the best possible light. Therefore, dressing is the perfect adjective for table.

Table is obvious for a chef, but it means so much more. The table is where the family gathers and where the food is served. Many emotions occur around a kitchen table. It is where feasts happen, where people celebrate a life after a death, and where weddings are planned. Even nightmares often are calmed through food at the kitchen table.

Families also sit around the table to discuss their lives and struggles. They plan for the future. They laugh, cry or yell. Families gather around the table for feasts and other events. In the past, families would gather for Sunday dinners. Although these events aren't as common today, they still happen, which makes the kitchen or dining room table an important part of people's lives. Food and recipes are important part of people's lives in all cultures. Food is a form of therapy and my love language. Many people show their love through food, but I always do because I am a chef.

In addition, dressing table has a more significant meaning for me and will give you a hint of the flavor of this cookbook. I had always placed my sister on a pedestal. I thought she was too perfect and too put together to be able to relate to me. I felt we weren't equal. One day, my sister called me out of the blue, which she never did. She was at an antique store and was looking at an antique dressing table, the place where women would sit and reflect on their lives while brushing their hair. My sister wanted my opinion on the table she was considering. I told her that I like dressing tables because of an episode of *I Love Lucy*. In the episode, Lucy sat at a dressing table, reading and eating chips. As she became engrossed in the story, she began dipping chips into her face cream. It was my favorite episode because I love eating chips and dip and could see myself making that mistake. My sister had surprised me then. She told me she liked that episode too and liked dressing tables for the same reason. Therefore, the dressing table became a way my sister and me could relate to each other. I now had a connection with my sister, and as mentioned earlier, dressing tables allow others to relate to people.

The final reason why *Dressing Table* is the title of my cookbook comes from my theory that women will sit before the dressing table, look in the mirror and reflect on their lives. I am reflecting on my life in this book and allowing others to see how we all experience struggles and joys in life that come from the table and food

Why I Am Writing This Book

I am not a writer. I am a chef. I believe that people can tell stories through food. I will provide you an experience through the world of cooking and my incredible recipes. We all go through life with joys, sorrows, struggles and experiences. In this book, you will see similar struggles you have faced reflected in my own life. It is about strong women, such as my mother, who at the age of 50 found herself divorced and alone. She didn't let that stop her. She continued to live. She raised us and moved us to Chantilly, Va., while commuting to her job in Maryland. She did what was necessary for us to survive. My mother walked a new path to redefine who she was when she no longer was a wife. This book is about my sister who lived alone with her daughter. It is about my friend who was a courageous businesswoman who ran a day care for more than 20 years. It is about their hopes, dreams, ambitions and struggles and the ones we all face as we go through our lives. It is about finding your identity and knowing who you are inside yourself.

While the book will highlight the women and their incredible strength. It will also talk about the men who have shown me who I am. For example, my husband has taken care of three families. He had an original family, but got divorced. I was single and raising my two kids. He helped me. Then we had a child together. All through this time, he did it God's way. My sons caused me heartache and joy at the same time. The book shows how raising a blended family and families in general could be hard. My son has attention deficit hyperactive disorder and oppositional defiance disorder. He was difficult to raise. It got to the point that I had to put him in a residential facility, which broke my heart. My second son had severe asthma, which caused a number of trips to the emergency room. Another heartache and joy came with my youngest son. He was born with a terrible bowel infection, but God saved his life. We all have to get through the hard times. This book will make you think about difficulties and how to survive them with food, family and God's love.

But, this book serves as a reminder that we are not alone. We always walk with God. When my mother commuted to Maryland for her job, she often faced traffic and weather that meant driving home wasn't safe. She would stay in Maryland, and I would be by myself in Virginia. I was never scared. I never felt like I was alone. I always believed someone was taking care of me. Even though I didn't know how to cook, I could sense someone tell me what to do. I knew what to remove from the refrigerator and what steps to take to create a meal. At night, I felt comforted. It took me so long to understand that it was the Lord. I never understood until much later that the Holy Spirit was guiding me on how to take care of myself and what to cook. God always took care of me my whole life. God is amazing. I wanted to show how God loves each of us. He is always with each of us. You never walk alone. God took care of me before I was born. He let me be born and found me several families who love me.

I wanted to discover who I was as a person. Through cooking I learned who I am and want to show how people can discover themselves through recipes. In my youth, I felt awkward because I knew I was adopted. I went on a journey to find my biological mother and learn my identity and how to deal with the difficulties I faced. I was always overweight and thought I couldn't be loved. I have low self-esteem and confidence, dyslexia and other disabilities, and am on the autism spectrum. This book is meant to build my confidence and overcome my disabilities and tell you to be confident too. You can overcome difficulties and be the person you are meant to be. I had to get through it every single day. Every day, I remind myself that God and my family love me. My mother wouldn't have commuted that long drive to ensure we had food on our table if she didn't love me. My husband loves me. This book celebrates my amazing life with all those people who love me.

The cookbook is a symbol that people can excel even if they don't think they can. We can't let disabilities define who we are. We excel despite them. For example, I wanted to go to college, but because of my dyslexia, I couldn't pass the spelling and English requirements to qualify. I went to cooking school and learned to put my hopes and dreams in cooking. This was what I was meant to do. I accomplished this skill and mastered it. I worked for Bon Appetite in Dunedin, Fla., where I met Peter Kreuzinger, my mentor and inspiration.

This cookbook is also about having the perfect pantry, the perfect refrigerator and the perfect cabinets. When you make an investment in your kitchen and your food, you are making an investment in yourself and an investment for future generations. Keep reading. Although the stories in this book are true, the names involved in the stories are changed to protect the individuals' privacy. So, experience the emotions involved with cooking and *bon appetite!*

APPETIZERS

APPETIZERS ARE PERFECT FOR LITTLE HANDS

The appetizers are traditionally served before the meal while guests are gathering and beginning small talk. This has always been the case. In history, people would gather in drawing rooms, sampling small foods before the main meals are served. They also tend to be served for Christenings and family get-togethers. Therefore, appetizers could be a metaphor for childhood. Parents often struggle with their children while, at the same time, children struggle with their growing years. All children try to find out who they should be. Often, they are unsure about themselves. It is sad that not all children are secure in their homes. They either have illnesses, disabilities or danger. Others are bullied at school or home. Some children bully others while at the same time get bullied. Schools also provide too much pressure. Food becomes therapy for many children as they get older. Parents help soothe the hurts with food as much as they listen to their children. However, parents don't always choose the correct path. They always are doing the best they can. As children struggle, they become more confident in who they are and who they want to be. The food becomes the way to find themselves just like appetizers are the way to know if people can anticipate a good meal.

Mary was born in July. She was two months premature, which might be a reason for her attention deficit disorder and dyslexia. She was diagnosed when she struggled in school. Her biological father didn't want the baby and filed to put the baby up for adoption. Mary's biological mother didn't know that this had happened, and she already had two daughters and was struggling financially. So Mary was put into a foster home who eventually adopted her. Mary's mother had a boy, Jaime, and a girl, Jessica. They became her siblings even though they all had different biological parents. Their parents couldn't have children of their own. Mary's mother worked for what was C&P Telephone before it became Verizon. They were happy until Mary's parents got divorced. Her mother was 50. Her father married the other woman. At age eight, Mary started on her path to love cooking. She created different foods, such as a chocolate cream pie with Hersey's chocolate. It wasn't good until she realized that it should have been made with unsweetened chocolate.

Because of the divorce, After the divorce, Mary's parents had to sell their home. Mary was 12. Her siblings were already out of the house with their own lives. During this time, Mary also struggled with her weight, her dyslexia and ADD. She was having trouble in school and felt that fellow students were making fun of her. Adding this stress on top of the stress of the divorce and moving didn't help her, but her mother did what she could to alleviate Mary's issues. They moved to Chantilly, Va., and lived in a mobile home. Her mother continued to work in Maryland, which forced her to have long commutes. Mary's mother didn't want to drive in the snow and had a boyfriend in Maryland. On these nights, she would stay in Maryland while Mary stayed in Virginia. Mary got through these stormy nights without her mother listening to John Denver music and cooking. She got into learning disability classes in Fairfax County, Va., which helped her begin to do well in school.

However, Mary's mother couldn't afford the Virginia taxes, so they had to move again. Mary had a relative in Clearwater, Fla. So, once again, in high school, Mary found herself moving to a strange place. The schools in

Florida didn't offer the same learning disability classes that Virginia did. She almost didn't graduate, but she did get her diploma. It was a struggle. She wanted to go to college, but she couldn't pass the Comp I English test, so she believed her dream of college was not going to happen.

Food became her love language. To help her mother, she would prepare dinner and other meals. She began making food for friends, relatives and others. She baked and cooked. She began to love recipes and learning about the flavors of food. Although her mother worked in offices in Florida, she decided to go to nursing school. Mary's mother suggested Mary attend Pinellas Technical College for Culinary Arts. Her professors understood her problem with taking tests and gave her oral tests. She was pregnant with her second child when she graduated with a culinary arts degree and became a chef. The day after she graduated with her degree, she started at Bon Appetite. She worked from 1989 to 2001. Now, she is sharing her recipes with other families.

(Appetizers: Small dish of food or a drink taken before a meal or a main course of a meal to stimulate one's appetite.)

Beef Nachos

Ingredients:

Two pounds of ground chuck

One and a half cups of water

Two envelopes of taco seasoning mix

One bag of tortilla chips

Four cups of shredded cheddar cheese

Two cups of shredded Monterey Jack cheese

¾ of a cup of Kalamata olives

Two small tomatoes

Large red onion, diced small

16 ounces of sour cream

Large head of romaine lettuce, sliced very thinly

Brown the ground beef in a Dutch oven. Drain off excess oil. Add water and taco seasoning mix. Simmer for 15 minutes, stirring occasionally. Take a large oven-safe platter. Add half of tortilla chips in single layer. Put meat mixture on top. Add half of cheddar and Monterey Jack cheeses on top. Repeat process. Put platter in preheated oven at 400 degrees. Wait until cheese starts to melt. Remove from oven. Add tomatoes, olives and onions. Add sour cream in dabs. Finish with shredded lettuce on top.

(For chicken nachos, use chicken instead of beef.)

Beef Tenderloin Canopies

Ingredients:

One long French *baguette*

A pound of center-cut *filet mignon (Chateaubriand)*

3/4 of a cup of good mayonnaise

One tablespoon of horseradish

One large sweet onion, thin sliced thin

Two tablespoons of salted butter

Salt and pepper for taste

Olive oil to coat bread

Cut baguette at angle. Make little crostinis. Place on 1/2 sheet pan. Sprinkle on olive oil, salt and pepper. Bake in oven of 375 degrees until golden brown. Remove to cool. Take *Chateaubriand* and pat dry. Rub meat with soften butter. Sprinkle with salt and pepper. Place in oven-safe baking dish and put in preheated oven at 375 degrees. Cook until internal temperature is 145 for medium or 150 for medium-well. In a medium saute pan on medium heat, add butter. When melted and sizzling, add onions, salt and pepper. Stir occasionally. Remove from heat once browned. In a small bowl, mix mayonnaise and horseradish. Spread mixture on crostinis. Once *Chateaubriand* has rested and is cold, slice thin. Place one slice on top of each crostini. Garnish with caramelized onion. Place on a decorative platter.

Coconut Shrimp

Ingredients:

Pound of large shrimp, shelled and deveined

1/2 cup of cornstarch

Half cup of coconut flour

Five large eggs

Eight-ounce can of coconut milk

Eight-ounce bag of unsweetened coconut

One cup of Panko bread crumbs

Two cups of coconut oil

Salt and pepper for taste

Set up a breading station. Put half a cup of cornstarch and half a cup of coconut flour in a small bowl. Whisk five large eggs in a separate bowl. Lightly add salt and pepper to flavor. Whisk again lightly. Mix Panko bread crumbs and unsweetened coconut in another small bowl. Lay shrimp on white paper towels and pat dry. Start to bread the shrimp in cornstarch and coconut flour mixture shaking off excess. Run shrimp through the egg mixture. Put shrimp through bread crumb mixture. Pat the mixture to the shrimp. Take a half sheet baking pan with rack. Place breaded shrimp on top of rack. This helps to dry mixture on shrimp. Heat coconut oil in deep-sided saute pan. Heat to 350 degrees using cooking thermometer. Brown shrimp on both sides till crispy. Take from pan and place on paper towel covered plate. Sprinkle on salt and then arrange on a platter with a small bowl of dipping sauce.

Ingredients for sauce:

Half a cup of orange marmalade

A quarter cup of Dijon mustard

Whisk to combine.

(*For Chicken Coconut, use same recipe. Substitute shrimp for chicken breast. Use one and a half pounds of chicken breasts, cut into bite-size pieces.*)

Fried Mozzarella Cheese Sticks

Ingredients:

24 mozzarella string cheese sticks

One and a half cups of flour

Quarter cup of cornstarch

Four large eggs

Half a cup of milk

Two cups of Italian-seasoned bread crumbs

Peanut oil

Use enough peanut oil to fill a six-quart Dutch oven halfway. Mix flour and cornstarch together in one bowl. In another bowl, mix eggs and milk together. In a third bowl, put bread crumbs. Heat Dutch oven with oil to 360 degrees. Place string cheese in freezer until almost frozen. Remove from freezer. Put cheese in flour and cornstarch mixture, then into egg and milk mixture and finally into bread crumbs. Let cheese rest on wire rack approximately 15 to 20 minutes while oil is heating to temperature. Place in Dutch oven. Brown evenly. Remove and drain onto paper towel-covered plate. Serve with marinara sauce.

Louise's Easy Dip

Ingredients:

Cut vegetables, a variety

Crackers, a variety

Good Seasons Mix

Eight-ounce container of sour cream

In a mixing bowl, pour sour cream. Add Good Seasons mix. Combine. Put into center of chip-and-dip tray. Surround dip with vegetables and crackers.

Poutine

(Poutine *is a dish that includes French fries and cheese curds topped with a brown gravy. It originated in the Canadian province of Quebec and emerged in the late 1950s.)*

Ingredients:

32-ounce bag of frozen French fries

Enough olive oil to sprinkle on French fries

Salt and pepper to taste

All purpose seasoning for taste

One pound of sirloin steak

One and 1/4 cup of all-purpose flour

Two cups of beef broth

Two pounds of cheese curds, broken apart

1/4 cup of whole milk

3/4 cup of beer

Two quarts of corn oil

Two large eggs

Arrange French fries on a half sheet baking pan in one layer. Sprinkle with olive oil, salt, pepper and seasoning salt. Place in a preheated 425-degree oven until golden brown. In a saute pan, add two tablespoons of olive oil, steak, salt and pepper to taste. Brown on both sides until medium-well. Remove steak from pan. Let rest. Add quarter cup of flour to drippings remaining in pan and gradually stir in beef broth until thickened. Add salt and pepper to taste. Reduce temperature to very low. Stir occasionally. In a medium-sized bowl, whisk together milk, one cup of flour, beer, half a teaspoon of salt and two eggs. Continue to whisk until it makes a thin batter. Add cheese curds to batter. Heat corn oil in a Dutch oven to 375 degrees. Shake off excess batter. Add cheese curds to Dutch oven. Brown for one to two minutes. Remove with wire strainer, called a spider. Drain onto paper towels. Sprinkle with salt. Remove French fries from oven. Arrange onto a large platter. Make sure gravy is thickened. Pour over French fries. Cut steak into small pieces against the grain. Apply steak on top of gravy. Put cheese curds on top.

Rebecca's Sauteed Mushrooms

Ingredients:

Two large packages of button mushrooms

Four tablespoons of butter

Quarter cup of low-sodium soy sauce

Salt and pepper to taste

Add butter to hot saute pan. Add mushrooms to pan. Saute until mushrooms start to get soft and tender. Add soy sauce, salt and pepper to taste. Once mushrooms are tender, remove. Put in serving bowl and serve immediately.

Salmon Canapes

Ingredients:

One French *baguette*

One quarter cup of olive oil

Salt and pepper for taste

Eight ounces of whipped cream cheese

12 slices of good smoked salmon

Two bunches of fresh dill

Half of red onion, chopped fine

One tablespoon of capers

Preheat oven to 375 degrees. Cut *baguettes* into crostinis. Place into half sheet baking pan. Sprinkle with olive oil, salt and pepper. Add to oven. Once browned, remove from oven. Let cool. Spread soften cream cheese on each crostini. Sprinkle little bit of onions, a few capers and a dill sprig on each crostini. Add 1/2 slice of salmon on each. Serve on two decorative platters.

Sauteed Mushrooms

Ingredients:

Two large packages of large button mushrooms

Four tablespoons of salted butter

Four cloves of minced garlic

Two tablespoons of finely chopped parsley

One tablespoon of Worcestershire sauce

Salt and pepper to taste

Use large hot skillet. Add butter. When it starts to sizzle, add mushrooms. Stir constantly. When mushrooms are soft, add Worcestershire sauce, salt and pepper to taste. Once mushrooms are softened, add parsley. Once mushrooms are tender, remove. Put in serving bowl and serve immediately.

Tomato Juice

(For Christmas and Thanksgiving, my mother would always start the meal off with a small glass of tomato juice. She always called it an appetizer. So I am putting it with the appetizers. Over the years, my sister and I have added things to the tomato juice. Sometimes, we turned it into a Bloody Mary by using Bloody Mary mix and vodka. We added skewers of chunk cheese, sausage, Genoa salami, pepperoni and summer sausage to the juice. Sometimes, we would put grilled kielbasa, green olives, limes and plenty of celery on the skewers in the juice. Sometimes, we had skewers of grilled shrimp. We like to fill it with a lot of interesting things. Have fun with it and be creative.)

Ingredients:

One can of good chilled tomato juice

Bloody Mary mix

One shot glass of vodka

Any of the skewers listed.

BREADS

THE DOCTOR IS PRESCRIBING BREAD

In restaurants, bread is served prior to the meal to allow patrons to get nourishment while waiting for appetizers or the entrees. Breads also serve as comfort foods. For example, when pregnant women are nauseated, they can eat toast. Or, after a stomach virus, people should eat toast until they can digest something else. Babies are given cereal or crackers before other foods. Breads are often served during holidays: An Easter bread or Christmas bread. Families will bring out breads during events usually ones cooked themselves. Northern countries and states use bread to build mass during cold winters. It is a nickname for money, and moldy bread helped a scientist to discover penicillin. In most cultures, families learn how to make breads to sustain life. For poor people, bread is the only option for food. In the Bible, manna is the bread that God sent the Israelites to sustain their lives in the desert. Jesus is the Bread of Life. He also is tempted to turn stones into bread, but He refuses. Thus, breads are an important food for living. Doctors also are important to people's lives. They heal and prevent death. They comfort when needed.

Mary had a fear of doctors because she was overweight and because a doctor contributed to her mother's death. She had no insurance. She received Social Security disability payments. One day, she was told to visit a doctor. A psychologist that was treating Mary suggested she see a doctor who went to medical school later in life. Mary was so anxious in the waiting room that she almost left, but she didn't. She decided to face her fears and see the doctor. He was nice and kind. He told her that he used to appraise homes, but he always had a dream to be a doctor. It took him 10 years, but he got his degree and medical license. "It's never too late for people to pursue their dreams. If you want to write a cookbook, you should do it," he told Mary. The doctor impressed Mary with his kindness. She had never believed that doctors could care about their patients. Most of the time, Mary thought they saw a patient for 15 minutes. However, Dr. Garrett Gauze would take time to talk with his patients and listen to them even if took a long time. He personally calls his patients and asks how they are doing after a visit or treatment. This is rare. Normally, a nurse will make those calls. Dr. Gauze also went above and beyond for his patients. One time, Mary was in Vineland, N.J., and had an urinary tract infection, but she couldn't find a hospital or urgent care facility. She needed a doctor to prescribe medicine. Mary called Dr. Gauze, who evaluated her symptoms over the phone. He called the pharmacy and provided his licensing information to the pharmacist in Vineland, so Mary could get her prescription and feel better.

He was her doctor until he got a job offer to be the medical director of Ideal Image. He has been with Ideal Image for 14 years.

The second doctor who influenced Mary was Dr. Cruz Faña-Souchet. Before she starts her day, she prays. She asks God for wisdom on how to treat her patients and guidance throughout the day. She is the founder of the AMA Medical Group and is certified in infectious diseases. She is known for using high quality evidenced-based measures and providing excellent care to her patients. She took care of Mary, making her feel at ease. Even when Mary sees other doctors she will ask Dr. Faña-Souchet for advice too. She often helped Mary with concerns over Solomon. Because Solomon was born after her mother died and because he was born with problems, she doubted her motherly instincts in raising him. She went to the doctor whenever Solomon showed symptoms of various illnesses. Dr. Faña-Souchet would allow her to come, and she would talk with Mary to calm her worries or soothe her fears. She also would recommend other doctors that would help Mary. And, she and Mary shared a love of family and friends. Dr. Faña-Souchet enjoys cultural activities, which usually involve food and fun. She remains a strong influence in Mary's life today.

The third doctor to inspire Mary was Dr. Robert Black. She began her relationship with him when Solomon was an infant. Mary shopped in the grocery store with the baby. Her left arm started to hurt and she was sweating. She thought she was having a heart attack. Dr. Faña-Souchet examined her. She recommended Mary see a cardiologist, Dr. Robert Black. He took heart tests and found out it was a panic attack, which often has similar symptoms. Because Mary was told to see him once a year, she has gotten to know him. He and Mary have much in common that has helped to ease her fear of doctors. His undergraduate degree is in zoology, and he loves animals. They bonded over their love for dogs. Dr. Black shows how much he cares for his patients. He often comes to the waiting room to ease patients' minds or to bring them to the examining room himself. Like Dr. Faña-Souchet he believes strongly in Jesus and cares for people. Today, these doctors continue to help Mary feel strong and healthy. She benefited from knowing them.

Dr. Andrew Saqua told Mary that she could write a cookbook if she wanted to do it. He worked with Dr. Faña-Souchet until his contract expired. He moved into doing telemedicine. Dr. Faña-Souchet told Mary to give her new doctor, Dr. Martin, a chance. He might surprise her. She took Dr. Faña-Souchet's advice. It turned out that Dr. Martin was 57 like Mary. He had three daughters to Mary's three sons. And, his patients are important to him. "I am here and focused on you."

(Bread: is a stable food prepared from a dough of flour and water, usually by baking. Throughout recorded history it has been a prominent food in many parts of the world and is one of the oldest man-made foods. It has had a significant importance since the dawn of agriculture.)

Blueberry Muffins

Ingredients:

One cup of all-purpose flour

Half a cup of whole wheat flour

Half a cup of sugar

Quarter cup of light brown sugar

One teaspoon of salt

Two teaspoons of baking powder

A third of a cup of vegetable oil

Two eggs

One third of a cup of milk

One and a half cups of fresh blueberries

One tablespoon of orange zest

Quarter cup of sugar in the raw

In a medium-sized mixing bowl, add all ingredients in order of list. Using cupcake wrappers, insert into a 12-cup pan. (*I like to spray the inside of the cup cake wrappers with a cooking spray.*) Pour batter into each cupcake wrapper until 2/3 full. Sprinkle with sugar in the raw on top of each cupcake. Place in preheated 375-degree oven for 20 to 25 minutes. Check by inserting toothpick in the center of each. Make sure it comes out clean. Remove and enjoy with lots of butter.

Brown Sugar Pecan Rolls

Ingredients:

One roll of Pillsbury flaky biscuit rolls

One and 1/2 cups of salted and melted butter

Two cups firmly packed light brown sugar

One cup of chopped pecans

Half a teaspoon of cinnamon

One cup of honey-butter

On a plate, add brown sugar, pecans and cinnamon. Blend together. Add butter to a saucepan. Over low heat, melt butter. Completely remove from heat. Take one biscuit at a time from the roll. Dip into butter. Roll into the sugar and nut mixture coating completely. Using a 9-inch pie pan, coat completely with butter. Place biscuits into pan. Place into oven. Bake according to package directions. Once baked, remove from oven. Cut into halves. Serve warm. Coat with honey-butter.

Chocolate Chip Bread

Ingredients:

One cup of salted butter, softened

Three-quarters of a cup of sugar

One cup of light brown sugar, packed

Four eggs

Two cups of sour cream

Two cups of all-purpose flour

One cup of cocoa powder

One tablespoon of baking powder

One tablespoon of salt

Two cups of semi sweet chocolate

In a medium-sized mixing bowl, whip together the butter and all the sugars. Continue to mix. Add eggs in one at a time. Mix well after each one. Add sour cream. Mix until creamy. Add all dry ingredients until well-blended. Using a wooden spoon, add one and 1/2 cups of the chocolate chips. Mix with spoon. Spoon batter into a well-greased bundt pan. Gently tap pan on counter to release any air bubbles that may be in it. Sprinkle remaining chips on top. Place in preheated 350-degree oven for 60 to 70 minutes until toothpick comes out clean. Remove from oven. Invert on a platter. Tap with a knife on all sides to release from pan. Remove from pan. Serve warm. Dust with powdered sugar and serve with butter.

Cinnamon Rolls

Ingredients:

Half a cup of water

Half a cup of whole milk

Two and a half teaspoons of active dry yeast

Quarter cup of sugar

Four tablespoons of unsalted butter, softened but slightly cooled

One and 1/2 cups of salted butter, softened

One large egg yolk

One and 1/2 teaspoons of vanilla extract

Two and 3/4 cups all-purpose flour plus more for dusting

One teaspoon of salt

Ingredients for cinnamon sugar:

One and a half cups of sugar

Two heaping tablespoons of cinnamon

Three-quarters of a cup of chopped pecans

Ingredients for Icing:

Four ounces of cream cheese, softened

14 tablespoons of salted butter, softened

One teaspoon of vanilla extract

Four tablespoons of milk

Three cups of powdered sugar, sifted

Half a teaspoon of salt

Heat water and milk in saucepan until a thermometer registers a 100 degrees Fahrenheit. Remove from heat. Sprinkle yeast on top. Sprinkle with a pinch of sugar on top. Set aside undisturbed until foamy. Usually, about five minutes. Add butter, egg yolk and vanilla extract into yeast mixture. Mix until combined. In a large bowl, whisk together flour, sugar and salt. Make a well in the center. Add yeast mixture. Stir with a wooden spoon to make a thick and slightly sticky dough. Turn dough out onto a floured surface and knead for six minutes. Make a ball from the dough. Take a larger bowl, smearing bowl with butter. Add dough into bowl, covering with plastic wrap and refrigerate overnight. Remove bowl from refrigerator. Turn flour onto a floured surface. Roll flat with a floured rolling pin. Roll into a long rectangle quarter inch thick. Smear one and a half cups of softened butter over surface of dough. In a small bowl, add the cinnamon, sugar and pecans. Blend together. Spread contents over the top of the buttered dough. (When I was advanced in cooking, my instructor had me sprinkle a cup and a half of frozen blueberries over top. It's optional but delicious.) Start with one end of the dough, rolling real tight. The more times you can roll it, the better it will be. Place dough on seamed side. Slice dough into about one and 1/2 in thick slices. Take a 9 by 13 baking dish. Butter all sides and bottom. Spread out your rolls, laying flat into pan. Set aside. Let them rise for about an hour. Brush with melted butter. Place into preheated 350-degree oven for about 35 to 40 minutes until rolls are golden brown and baked through the center. Remove from oven.

In a medium mixing bowl, add cream cheese and butter. Using mixer, blend together until creamy. Add milk. Continue to mix. Add salt and vanilla extract. Mix until all is blended. Mix and slowly add powdered sugar. When it becomes a thick, glaze consistency, pour over warm rolls. Enjoy.

Cornbread

Ingredients:

Two cups of all-purpose flour

Two cups of cornmeal

One and 1/3 cups of sugar

Two teaspoons of salt

Two and 1/2 tablespoons of baking powder

Three eggs

Two cups of milk

2/3 cup of vegetable oil

Two tablespoons of sour cream

Preheat oven to 375 degrees. Using a large cast iron skillet, place on burner on medium-high with two tablespoons of shortening. Heat until shortening is melted and sizzling. Take off heat. In a large mixing bowl, combine all ingredients in order listed. Mix well. Pour contents into skillet. Place skillet in oven. Bake until toothpick inserted in center comes out clean. Serve with a lot of butter and honey. Delicious.

Herb Dinner Rolls

Ingredients:

Six cups of all-purpose flour

Three tablespoons of granulated sugar

Four and 1/2 teaspoons of yeast

Two teaspoons of salt

One and 1/2 cups of water

Half a cup of milk

One teaspoon of fresh chopped parsley

One teaspoon of chopped fresh oregano

One teaspoon of chopped fresh rosemary

One teaspoon of chopped fresh basil

Two tablespoons of salted butter, softened

For glazing: three-quarters of a cup of melted butter

Four garlic cloves, minced

Half a cup of grated Parmesan cheese

Using a standing mixer, put into bowl two cups of flour, sugar, dry yeast, salt and spices. Mix until blended. Using a microwavable safe bowl, add water, milk and butter. Microwave for 15 seconds at a time until reaching temperature of 120 degrees. Add contents to flour mix. Beat for two minutes on medium speed. Gradually, add one cup of flour. Beat for another two minutes, scraping bowl. Stir in enough flour so contents form a ball. Knead on floured surface until smooth and elastic, approximately six to eight minutes. Let rest for about 10 minutes. In a 9 by 13 cooking pan, spray a good amount of cooking spray. Then divide dough into 16 equal balls. Place in pan. Put a towel over it. Let it rest for 45 minutes. Place pan in a preheated 450-degree oven and bake until rolls are golden brown. Check within 20 to 30 minutes. Remove from oven. Turn pan gently upside down, releasing rolls from pan. Turn rolls to other side. Make glaze for top of rolls. Add minced garlic cloves to melted butter. Using a pastry brush, brush ingredients over top of rolls. Sprinkle with fresh grated Parmesan cheese and serve warm.

Homemade Pita Bread

Ingredients:

Two teaspoons of active dry yeast

Three-quarters of a teaspoon of sugar

Two cups of whole wheat flour

Three-quarters of a cup of all-purpose flour

One teaspoon of Kosher salt

One cup of lukewarm water

Add water into large mixing bowl. Add yeast and sugar.
Stir in one quarter cup of whole wheat flour and all of
the all-purpose flour. Blend together. Set aside bowl with
ingredients uncovered until you see yeast is blooming. Add
salt, olive oil and one and 1/4 cups of whole wheat flour.
Mix with wooden spoon until blended. Dust with flour.
Knead for one minute. Add dough to floured surface. Knead
again for two minutes. Cover dough. Let rest for 10 minutes.
Knead again for another two minutes. The dough should
be soft and a bit moist. Transfer dough into a Ziploc bag.
Place in refrigerator overnight. The next day, remove from
refrigerator and let it rest. Bring it to room temperature.
Knead into a ball. Place in a clean bowl. Cover bowl tightly
with plastic wrap. Place a towel over top. Place bowl in a
warm spot in kitchen for one hour. Preheat oven to 475
degrees. Place a half baking sheet in oven. Take bowl with
dough and punch down into bowl to allow air to escape
from dough. Divide dough into eight even parts. Form
pieces into balls. Place the dough balls on counter and place
a damp kitchen towel over top for 10 minutes. Remove one
of the dough balls and place onto lightly floured counter.
Taking a floured rolling pin, roll into a six-inch circle about
1/8 inch thick. Dust flour if needed, doing the same to the
other pieces. Place all pieces on a hot baking sheet. And
place back in oven for two minutes. Turn with a spatula.
Bake another minute. When ready, you will notice a few
brown spots. Place in a bread basket with a towel. (*I like to
serve it with basil pesto for dipping or cut in half and filled
with chicken or tuna salad.*)

Louise's Lemon Bread

Ingredients:

One cup sugar plus 1/3 cup sugar

One and half cup flour

Six tablespoons butter

One teaspoon salt

Two eggs, slightly beaten

One teaspoon baking powder

Half cup milk

Rind of one lemon

Juice from one lemon

Preheat oven to 350 degrees. Grease loaf pan. Melt butter, one cup of sugar and eggs. Sift flour, salt and baking powder. Add dry ingredients to egg mixture, alternating with milk. Beat well. Add lemon rind. Mix well. Bake one hour. Remove from oven. Cool. While cooling, mix lemon juice and one-third cup sugar. While bread is hot, pour lemon mixture over the top.

SOUPS

BLENDING RIGHT SOUP FLAVORS
TAKES TIME TO MASTER

To make a chowder, soup or bisque, you need many different ingredients and flavors. While some soups blend well, such as Italian wedding soup that combines both chicken and beef flavors into the broth, others, such as pumpkin soup, are better off with one flavor. As a chef, learning how to combine flavors is a skill that could be mastered, combining personalities in a family structure doesn't always work. However, parents do their best and try to resolve the struggles of blending a family. Listen to this family's struggles to remind you that you are not alone in your problems. Others understand and could help.

When Mary and Joseph got married. He had his kids. She had her kids. Then, Mary conceived. The family became, her kids, his kids and their kid, but the children were jealous of each other and their half brother. The children never got along. When they were married, it displaced them in the order of the household. He had an oldest one; and Mary had an oldest one. Mary's son was older than Joseph's elder child. In addition, Joseph had to fight in court over custody of his two children, which caused more friction and stress.

The children believed one parent favored Joseph's kids more or Mary's kids more or Solomon more. The five children and the two parents never felt like a family to anyone. The children did what was natural to kids. They pitted the parents against each other. When trying to blend personalities, the problem comes from the fact that Joseph was more emotionally involved with his kids and Mary was more emotionally involved with her kids.

To resolve these family issues, they went to family counseling. They tried everything that they felt they could do. Nothing seemed to work.

Although Mary and Joseph thought they would be able to bring all parties in the family together, in reality, it was hard to accomplish it. Mary often thought that the only perfect blended family was *The Brady Bunch*. Mary and Joseph took steps to do things together and be there for each other, but it always remained her kids versus his kids. His kids would say that they cared more about her kids while her kids would say they cared more about his kids. They all said the parents cared more about Solomon than any of them. No one could get along, and there was always constant conflict.

Besides family counseling, they invited in-home therapists to help the situation. They asked for help and followed the directions of mental health counseling. In the end, the children wouldn't accept the change in their situation.

His kids didn't like that Mary took on the mother role because they had a mother. They resented Mary because she took them away from their mother. Mary's kids didn't like Joseph at first as the father figure because they were fine without a father. Mary's sons didn't have a relationship with their father. As a result, they began to love Joseph and still do until this day, but that didn't help alleviate the situation. Despite the years and love that Mary and Joseph have imparted to all their children, the family remains divided to this day. Despite the times Mary used food to heal the family and bring them together, the family didn't get along.

All of the children are grown and adults living their lives now. His kids still think Mary and Joseph love her kids more. Poor Solomon remained in the middle. That is a hard situation for him. Even through all this adversity, Joseph and Mary's love story continues and grows stronger.

Whenever Mary got upset about the children and the conflict resulting from blending personalities, he would sing to her. He would sing, "We are standing on holy ground. There are angels all around. Let us praise Jesus now standing in his presence on holy ground."

They have endured challenges trying to raise the three families. They have tried to bring everyone together. It still doesn't work even though they are grown adults. His kids think her kids come first. Her kids think his come first. The situation is heart-breaking because Mary loves all five of them. She has always considered all of them to be her kids. Some of them won't talk to Mary. Every night, Mary prays that God will heal the family and that all five kids will be united.

Mary and Joseph miss her grandkids, born of his children. Mary hopes the children all realize that she still loves them, and she doesn't like having a broken family. In the past, Mary and Joseph would get together with the children on Thanksgiving, Christmas and Easter. It was a joyous time with the family when all of them were together.

During the times of their growth, they had family events, birthday parties and other special occasions. Those occasions are no longer happening and the parents miss them. Through all the trials, Mary and Joseph supported each other and kept going. Mary has heard from others who have tried to blend families and got similar results. Parents have to keep praying and believe that God will heal families in His time. And, rely on their love for each other to get them through the troublesome times.

(Soup: A liquid dish typically made by boiling meat, fish or vegetables in stock or water. I like using an oven method rather than trying to cook the soups on a stove, which could cause burns or a scorching taste.)

Baked Taco Soup

Two pounds of ground chuck

One large sweet onion

Six cloves of garlic, minced

Two packages of taco seasoning mix

One can of fire roasted diced tomatoes

One quart of beef broth

One teaspoon of chili powder

One teaspoon of smoked paprika

One teaspoon of cumin

Salt and pepper to taste

Eight ounces of large macaroni

Eight ounces of shredded cheddar cheese

One cup of prepared guacamole

16 ounces of sour cream

Half a cup of sliced green onion

Brown ground beef in a six-quart Dutch oven. Add diced onion, cooking until sweated. Add salt, pepper and other spices. Add garlic. Cooking until warm. Add diced tomatoes and quart of beef broth. Stir. Place lid and put in preheated oven at 325 degrees for about an hour and half, stirring every 20 minutes. Remove and stir in macaroni. Place back into oven for 20 minutes. Pour into serving bowls. Add dollops of guacamole, sour cream, cheddar cheese and green onions.

Beef Chili

Ingredients:

Two pounds of ground chuck

One large sweet onion, diced fine

Two large green peppers, diced medium

Two cans of dark red kidney beans

One can of crushed tomatoes

One can of fire-roasted diced tomatoes

One tablespoon of chili powder

One teaspoon of cumin

One teaspoon of coriander

Salt and pepper to taste

One quart of beef broth

16 ounces of sour cream

Eight ounces of shredded cheddar cheese

Two cups of cooked white rice

One cup of green onions, sliced

In a six-quart Dutch oven, brown ground chuck. Drain

all excess juice. Add sweet onions, green pepper, salt and pepper to taste. Cook to sweat. Add kidney beans, crushed tomatoes, diced tomatoes. Add one quart of beef broth. Stir in spices. Keep stirring. Place lid over chili. Place in preheated oven at 325 degrees for an hour and half, stirring every 20 minutes. Remove from oven. Place into dishes. Add rice, cheddar cheese, green onions and sour cream.

Black Bean Soup

Ingredients:

One bag of dried black beans emptied into a bowl of cool water covering beans, and let stand overnight

Two or three ham hocks

Six stalks of celery, chopped

Six carrots chopped

Two quarts of chicken broth

One teaspoon of cumin

Salt and pepper to taste

One bay leaf

Half a teaspoon of cardamom

One teaspoon of basil

One teaspoon of thyme

Four tablespoons salted butter

Eight ounces of sour cream

Two cups of cooked white rice

Eight ounces of cheddar cheese

One tablespoon of chili powder

One cup green onions, sliced thin

Add oil to heated Dutch oven. Add onion, celery, carrots, salt and pepper. Add seasonings and spices. Add chili powder. Drain and rinse beans. Add to Dutch oven. Pour two quarts of chicken broth over mixture. Gently add ham hocks. Cover pot and placed in preheated oven at 325 degrees for three hours, stirring every 20 minutes. When beans are tender, remove from oven. Place on stove. Gently remove ham hocks. Use potato masher to mash some but not all of the beans. This will help to thicken soup. Stir gently. Add butter. Put in serving bowls. Add white rice, sour cream, cheddar cheese and sliced green onions.

Butternut Squash Soup

Ingredients:

Two tablespoons of olive oil

One medium yellow onion, diced fine

One butternut squash, peeled, seeded and diced into big chunks

1/4 cup brown sugar, packed

Half teaspoon of nutmeg

Two quarts of chicken broth

Salt and pepper to taste

Four tablespoons of salted butter

Half a cup of heavy cream

Sour cream and parsley for garnishing

Add oil to six-quart Dutch oven on medium heat. Add onion and cook until sweating. Add chunks of butternut squash. Start cooking. Add brown sugar, nutmeg, salt and pepper to taste. When everything is starting to cook and blend, put in chicken stock. Cover and place in a preheated oven for 325 degrees for an hour to hour and a half until butternut squash is fork tender. Remove from the oven. In a blender, blend until soup is completely smooth. Add half cup of heavy cream and butter. Stir gently until everything is incorporated into the soup and soup is hot. Pour into serving bowls and dollop with sour cream and parsley.

Cabbage Soup

Ingredients:

Half a cup of olive oil

One large sweet onion, diced small

Six carrots, diced large

Six stalks of celery, diced fine

One whole head of cabbage, cored and diced into small pieces

Two quarts of chicken stock

One can of diced tomatoes

Two cups of diced ham

Four large peeled and diced potatoes

Salt and pepper to taste

Half a teaspoon of caraway seeds

Four chicken bouillon cubes

Teaspoon of basil

Teaspoon of oregano

Teaspoon of thyme

Add olive oil to a Dutch oven on medium heat. Add ham. Get some brown color on the ham. Add onions, carrots and celery. Cook until sweaty. Add salt, pepper and all spices until hot. Add in cabbage. Stir wait until cabbage wilts. Add tomatoes, chicken stock and bouillon cubes. Place in preheated oven at 325 degrees for hour and half, stirring every 20 minutes. Remove from oven. Serve immediately. (*I like to put a pad of butter on top.*)

Chicken Chili

Same as beef chili but substitute chicken for beef

Cut chicken into small chunks. Brown and drain. *Follow steps for beef chili.*

Chicken Noodle Soup

Ingredients:

Half a cup of olive oil

Salt and pepper for taste

Small chicken cut into eight pieces (no need for back or gizzards)

One large sweet onion, diced

Six carrots, diced

Eight stalks of celery, diced

Half teaspoon of turmeric

Four chicken bouillon cubes

Two bay leaves

One teaspoon of thyme

Two garlic cloves, minced

Half teaspoon of coriander

Two quarts of water

One bag of old-fashioned egg noodles

Add oil into heated six-quart Dutch oven. Add half of chicken, salt and pepper. Brown well on all sides in oil. Remove chicken from pot. Place on plate. Add onions, carrots and celery. Let sweat. Add salt and pepper to taste. Add all spices and chicken broth. Put chicken back in soup. Put into Dutch oven and replace lid. Place in preheated oven at 325 degrees for an hour and half. Check and stir every 20 minutes. While cooking, prepare noodles by boiling water. When boiling, add noodles. Don't cook all the way, about 10 minutes. Remove Dutch oven from oven. Remove chicken from pot with two forks. Take off skin and carefully remove chicken from bones. Place chicken back into pot. Place pot on stove. Turn on burner to medium. Once it starts to boil, add in cooked noodles. Serve immediately.

Chicken Rice Soup

See recipe for Chicken Noodle Soup. Replace noodles with two cups of cooked white rice.

Chili Mac

See recipe for beef chili.

Add cooked al dente elbow macaroni tossed in together. Pour into 9 by 13 baking dish and cover with lots of shredded cheddar cheese. Preheat oven to 375 degrees. Bake until hot and bubbly. The cheese should be melted and browned.

Cream of Potato Soup

Ingredients:

Half a cup of olive oil

Large sweet onion, diced fine

Five pounds of potatoes, peeled and diced medium

Two cups of chicken broth

Salt and pepper to taste

Two cups of half and half

Six stalks of celery, chopped fine

Six tablespoons of salted butter

Four garlic cloves

Eight ounces of shredded cheddar cheese

Eight slices of cooked and finely chopped bacon

Half a cup of sliced green onions

Add olive oil to six-quart heated Dutch oven. Add onions and celery. Heat until sweated. Add potatoes. Stir ingredients. Add chicken broth. Add garlic cloves. Stir well. Place lid on Dutch oven. Put into a preheated oven of 325 degrees for one hour. Potatoes should fall apart and be tender. Remove from oven. Put in blender and chill. Add butter and half and half. Put into bowls. Garnish with sour cream, bacon, cheddar cheese and onion. Add a little cracked black pepper.

Cream of Tomato Soup

Ingredients:

Two tablespoons of olive oil

One sweet whole onion, diced fine

Salt and pepper to taste

Four large cans of diced tomatoes

Half a teaspoon of basil

Half a teaspoon of thyme

Half a teaspoon of oregano

One quart of chicken broth

Six tablespoons of salted butter

Two cups of half and half

Add olive oil to heated six-quart Dutch oven. Add onion. Let it sweat. Add spices, salt and pepper. Heat to boiling. Add tomatoes and chicken broth. Place lid over Dutch oven and place in preheated 325 degrees for approximately one hour. Remove from the oven. Blend in blender until smooth. Stir in butter. Add in half and half. Serve immediately. (*It's fun to drizzle over the top a jar of prepared pesto sauce.*)

Italian Wedding Soup

Ingredients:

One pound ground chuck

Two slices of whole wheat bread

Two onions -- one grated, one cut fine

1/4 cup of ketchup

One quarter cup of Parmesan cheese, grated

Quarter cup of ricotta cheese

Salt and pepper to taste

Half a cup of olive oil

One pound and a half of cut raw chicken

Six stalks of celery, cut fine

One teaspoon oregano

One teaspoon basil

One large head of escarole

Quarter cup of whole milk

Four minced garlic cloves

Two large eggs

Two chicken bouillon cubes

One teaspoon of thyme

One teaspoon of ground rosemary

One teaspoon of herb of Provence

Add oil to heated six-quart Dutch oven. Add chicken. Cook until brown. Drain, leaving chicken in the Dutch oven. Add celery, cut onions and carrots. Cook until sweaty. Add salt and pepper to taste. Add other seasonings. Add bouillon cubes to warm water and boil. Make two quarts of chicken stock and add to other mixture. Stir constantly. Add lid to Dutch oven. Place in preheated oven of 325 degrees for an hour and a half, stirring every 20 minutes.

While soup is cooking, add ground chuck to medium-sized bowl. Add wheat bread on top of ground chuck. Cover bread with milk. Add eggs, grated onions, ketchup, salt and pepper, Parmesan cheese and ricotta cheese. With clean and dry hands, gently incorporate all ingredients. Do not over mix. This will cause tough meatballs. Take half baking sheet. Add parchment paper over cooking sheet. Measure out tablespoons of meat mixture. Roll into small meatballs until all mixture is used. Place on top of parchment paper. Bake for 30 minutes. Remove meatballs from oven. When Dutch oven time has expired, remove Dutch oven from stove. Place all meatballs in soup. Put Dutch oven on burner on medium heat. While soup is cooking, boil water and add a half box of orzo pasta. Boil for 10 minutes. Remove from heat. Add to soup. Place in washed chopped head of escarole. Stir and heat until greens are completely wilted. Serve and top with grated Parmesan cheese. (*You can use ground chicken ground turkey or ground pork instead of ground chuck for the meatballs.*)

Louise's Pumpkin Soup

(*My father always took the pumpkins from Halloween, cut them and pureed the meat of them. I started doing that too, but I needed to find a way to use up all the pumpkin besides pumpkin pies. This was one way I used my pumpkin. If you freeze your pumpkin, the water will be in the pumpkin and no additional water is needed.*)

Ingredients:

16 ounces of pureed pumpkin

Three tablespoons of butter

Three tablespoons of sugar

Salt and pepper to taste

Four cups boiling milk

Croutons

Add pumpkin to large pot. Add butter, sugar, salt and pepper. Let simmer for 15 minutes, stirring occasionally. Add milk, stirring well while pouring it in the pot. Cook 10 minutes. Be careful not to scald the milk. When well heated, pour over croutons in bowls.

Mom's Hamburger Soup

Ingredients:

Two pounds of ground chuck

One medium-sized sweet yellow onion, chopped

Four carrots, chopped

Six stalks of celery chopped

One 16-ounce can of diced tomatoes

Four medium-sized potatoes, peeled and chopped medium

One small frozen bag of mixed vegetables

Three quarts of beef broth

Three beef bouillon cubes

Salt and pepper to taste

One teaspoon of oregano

One teaspoon of basil

One teaspoon of thyme

Four garlic cloves minced

Four tablespoons of salted butter

Eight ounces of dried uncooked elbow macaroni

In a six-quart Dutch oven, add ground chuck and brown it. Leave all juices in the pot. Add carrots, celery and onion. Add all spices, herbs and garlic. Heat everything until all ingredients blend together. Add tomatoes and bag of vegetables. Stir until hot. Add in bouillon cubes and pepper to taste. Cover with lid. Put in preheated 325-degree oven for three hours, checking every half hour and stirring. Remove from the oven. Add in uncooked elbow macaroni. Stir ingredients. Put back in the oven for another 20 minutes. Remove from oven. Add four tablespoons of butter and stir. Pour into serving bowls and serve with Parmesan cheese sprinkled on top.

Mom's Navy Bean Soup

Ingredients:

One pound bag of dry navy beans

One ham bone

Six slices of bacon fried crisp and chopped

One can fire roasted diced tomatoes

One sweet yellow onion diced fine

Two dill pickles, diced fine

Four medium-sized potatoes, diced small

Six carrots, diced small

Two quarts of chicken broth

Quarter cup of olive oil

Four stalks of celery, diced small

One teaspoon oregano

One teaspoon of basil

Four cloves of garlic, minced

One teaspoon of thyme

One teaspoon of chopped fresh parsley

One teaspoon of ground cumin

Two cups of diced ham

Place navy beans in bowl with cool water. Cover and let
stand overnight. In large Dutch oven, add olive oil. Let it get

hot. Add onions, celery and carrots. Add salt and pepper to taste. Stir constantly while you're sweating the vegetables. Add in potatoes. Cook contents until all are nicely sweated. Add bacon, garlic, herbs and spices. Stir and let them get warm so that they can bloom. Add tomatoes. Next rinse and drain navy beans. Add beans to pot. Add chicken broth, pickles and gently add in ham bone. If ham bone is not available, you can try using two or three ham hocks. Also add two cups of diced ham. After everything is added, put lid on Dutch oven. Place in oblong half sheet pan. Place in preheated oven at 325 degrees for three hours, checking every half hour to stir. Remove from oven and gently take out ham bones. Discard bones. Stir and serve.

New England Clam Chowder

Ingredients:

Six slices of bacon, fried crispy and chopped

One sweet yellow onion, chopped fine

Six stalks of celery, chopped fine

Four potatoes, peeled and chopped medium

Three 16-ounce cans of clam pieces, undrained

Two quarts of chicken broth

Salt and pepper to taste

Six tablespoons of salted butter

A cup of water

1/4 cup all-purpose flour

Two cups of half and half

Add bacon into six-quart Dutch oven. Add onions and celery and let sweat. Add salt and pepper to taste. Add in potatoes. Start this cooking at medium heat. Add in clams with juices. Stir in chicken broth. Let simmer until a rolling boil. In a separate bowl, add cup of water and flour. Whisk together until there are no lumps. Gently pour into the slurry of the clam chowder. Keep stirring until it gets thickened. Add in two cups half-and-half. Add in your butter. Reduce heat to low. Serve immediately.

Split Pea Soup

Ingredients:

Half a cup of olive oil

One cup of diced ham

One large sweet onion, diced fine

Six carrots, diced fine

Six celery stalks, diced fine

One bag of dried split peas

Three quarts of chicken broth

Four garlic cloves, minced

Salt and pepper to taste

One bay leaf

Six tablespoons of butter

Add oil to heated six-quart Dutch oven. Add ham. Brown evenly. Add onions, carrots and celery. Cook until sweaty. Add salt, pepper and bay leaf. Stir in peas. When everything is added, put in the chicken broth. Place lid over oven and a place in preheated oven of 325 degrees for hour and a half, stirring every 20 minutes. Once peas are cooked, remove from oven and add butter. Place in soup bowls.

Sweet Potato Soup

Ingredients:

Eight large sweet potatoes, peeled and diced into large chunks

Cook sweet potatoes. *Follow steps to the recipe for Butternut Squash Soup.* Substitute sweet potatoes for the squash.

SALADS

SALADS GO WITH ENTREES
LIKE SIBLINGS IN FAMILIES

It takes many vegetables and ingredients to make tasty salads. The same is true for families. Many people and many personalities make up a family. The struggles that one family member has often impacts another member or the family as a whole. At the same time, joys of one member are shared by other members and the family unit as a whole. Sometimes, salads come with flavors that are not liked. You have to continue eating until you get to those vegetables you do like. Life is like that. You often have to follow a path that you don't like to come to a place of happiness. The road is not always a straight shot to the happy ending. Sometimes, you have to meander a long time before coming to the right spot where love and happiness flows. That was the case for Jessica and Jaime. Their path to happiness was crooked, but they eventually reached their happy ending.

Mary's siblings were quite a bit older than she was. Jessica, her sister, was seven years older, and Jaime, her brother, was 11 years older. Because Jessica and Jaime were closer in age, they spent more time together, mostly playing with other neighborhood children. They spent many snowy day, sledding on the neighborhood hills. The family had only one television, so what little time they had to watch, was spent together. After high school , Jaime got married and had a baby girl. When Jessica graduated, she began working for C&P Telephone and moved in with Jaime and his little family, leaving Mary alone with very dysfunctional parents. At the telephone company, Jessica met her husband, but not before marrying someone else first. As they aged, the marital relationship disintegrated and resulted in divorce. Jessica married, and eventually, the two older siblings lived close together and their children played together. Mary and their mother moved from place to place, eventually ending up in Florida. As time progressed, all the siblings moved to Florida, though not in the same city. Mary lived with their mother, and the siblings would visit often. Through the years, the siblings grew apart, as the miles and their lives took them on separate journeys. The girls found their forever mates and settled down in different cities. Their brother, Jaime, settled where their father had married, retired and eventually passed away. Their mother went through many life changes but never remarried. She had a few medical setbacks and lost her life immediately after bypass surgery. She left the three siblings lost without their mother.

After both Jessica and her husband left the phone company, they traveled for a few years. Then, they wanted to live where they could have four seasons because the Florida weather was becoming unbearable. They moved to East Tennessee where they found the perfect house for them. They now spend their days enjoying the beautiful scenery in Tennessee. While it wasn't easy for Jessica, she found her place of happiness.

Mary's borther Jaime was 11 years older than her but was always helpful. In her youth, Jaime lived in his mother's house with his pregnant girlfriend. When Mary's father and mother divorced, Mary moved to a mobile home in Virgina. Jaime and his girlfriend also moved to Virginia. Afer a few years, Jaime's wife had another daughter. They moved to Laurel, Md., because they needed more space. Mary spent summers with Jaime and his wife when she was in school.

When Mary and her mother moved to Florida, Jaime stayed in Maryland for two years. Then, he moved his family to Florida too. Jaime divorced the mother of his children. Mary didn't get along with his new girlfriend or his second wife, This put a strain between Mary and Jaime. Many years passed without them talking with each other much. During this time, Jaime went to truck-driving school and became a commercial driver. He drove a truck until he retired. Mary saw him again at their father's funeral. They struck up their friendship and sibling love at that time. After the funeral, Mary needed to fix her car, but she didn't have money for the specific parts she needed. Jaime offered her the money to fix her car.

Jessica and her husband discovered that they were both adopted. After their respective parents had passed away, they decided to test their DNA and try to get answers to their lifelong questions. After sharing this with Mary, she also decided to go down that path. After much research, they all found who their biological parents were and that many siblings were made. The three adopted children remain close and talk often.

(Salads: a cold dish of various mixtures of raw or cooked vegetables usually seasoned with oil, vinegar or other dressings It is sometimes accompanied by meat, fish or other ingredients.)

Chicken Salad

Ingredients:

Six chicken breast halves

Two tablespoons of olive oil

Salt and pepper to taste

Eight stalks of celery, chopped fine

One half of a small red onion, chopped fine

Three-quarters of a cup of pecans or almonds toasted in the oven and chopped fine

Half a cup of dried cranberries

Three quarters of a cup of good mayonnaise

Salt and pepper to taste

Half cantaloupe, seeded

Toasted coconut

Place chicken breasts on baking sheet sprayed with cooking spray. Brush olive oil on chicken breasts. Season with salt and pepper. Place in preheated oven at 350 degrees for 20 to 25 minutes or until chicken is cooked. Remove from oven and let cool. Shred with two forks and place in medium-sized bowl. Add celery, onions, nuts, cranberries, mayonnaise, salt and pepper. (*It is delicious to put inside a half of a seeded cantaloupe. Put toasted coconut on top It is wonderful to make for a fancy luncheon.*)

Coleslaw

Ingredients:

One large jicama cabbage, peeled and finely shredded

Half napa cabbage, finely shredded

Four carrots, finely shredded

One and a half cups of good mayonnaise

Half a cup of sugar

Two tablespoons of red wine vinegar

One teaspoon of celery salt

Salt and pepper to taste

Place jicama cabbage and carrots in a medium-sized bowl. In a small bowl, add mayonnaise, sugar, celery salt, vinegar, salt and pepper. Whisk gently. Add all ingredients into first bowl and toss well.

Louise's Sunshine Salad

One three-ounce package of lemon-flavored gelatin

One cup boiling water

Half cup cold water

1/8 teaspoon salt

One eight-ounce can of crushed pineapples with syrup

Half cup of shredded carrots

In a small bowl, add gelatin. Pour in boiling water. Stir until gelatin is dissolved. Add cold water, salt and pineapple with syrup. Chill until mixture is slightly thickened. Add carrots to gelatin mixture. Pour into a four-cup mold or baking pan (8 x 8 x 2). Chill until set. Serve salad in the mold or cut into squares. (*I have often chilled this in the bowl and served directly from bowl.*)

Mom's Kidney Bean Salad

Ingredients:

Two 16-ounce cans dark red kidney beans, drained and rinsed

Six hard-boiled eggs, peeled and diced

One small jar gherkin pickles, drained and chopped fine

Three-quarters of a cup of olive oil

One third cup of apple cider vinegar

One quarter cup of sugar

Salt and pepper to taste

In medium bowl, add kidney beans, hard boiled eggs and pickles. Mix together. Add remaining ingredients. Mix. Serve.

Mom's Macaroni Salad

Ingredients:

One pound box of elbow macaroni

One green pepper, diced small

One red pepper, diced small

One yellow pepper, diced small

One red onion, diced small

Two cups of Miracle Whip salad dressing

One eight-ounce container of Parmesan cheese

Half cup of whole milk

Salt and pepper to taste

Two tablespoons of apple cider vinegar

Two tablespoons of yellow mustard

Cook macaroni *al dente*. Drain and cool into large bowl. Add peppers and onions. Mix together. In medium-sized bowl, add Miracle Whip salad dressing. Add milk, vinegar, mustard, salt and pepper. Whisk to combine. Pour into macaroni mixture. Toss to combine and coat the macaroni and vegetables. Sprinkle on container of Parmesan cheese and toss. If contents are too stiff, add milk to loosen. (*It is delicious to add diced ham to salad or shredded cooked chicken or two cans of tuna fish drained.)*

Mom's Potato Salad

Ingredients:

Five pounds of rustic potatoes, peeled, diced and boiled

Two cups of Miracle Whip salad dressing

Eight hard-boiled eggs, peeled and diced

One small jar of gherkin pickles, drained and chopped fine

Two tablespoons of yellow mustard

One medium red onion, diced fine

One tablespoon of sugar

One tablespoon of apple cider vinegar

Salt and pepper to taste

In large bowl, add cooled and drain potatoes. Add hard boiled eggs, onions and gherkin pickles. Toss ingredients together. In a separate medium bowl, add Miracle Whip salad dressing, sugar, vinegar and mustard. Whisk to combine. Add salt and pepper. Pour ingredients over potato mixture and toss together. If ingredients are too thick pour in whole milk until you are satisfied.

Salmon Salad

See recipe for tuna salad. Replace tuna fish for 12 ounces of cooked and flaked salmon.

Three Bean Salad

Ingredients:

One can of green beans, drained

One can of wax beans, drained

One can of dark red kidney beans, drained

One large green pepper, diced fine

One large red pepper, diced fine

One medium red onion, diced fine

Three-quarters of a cup of olive oil

1/3 cup apple cider vinegar

Half a cup of sugar

Salt and pepper to taste

Add three cans of beans to medium-sized bowl. Add peppers and onions. Toss. In separate small bowl, add olive oil, vinegar, sugar, salt and pepper. Whisk ingredients well. Combine all ingredients together from both bowls. Mix well. (*I like to make that and then add some to a green salad. It's delicious.*)

Trough Salad

Ingredients:

One head of romaine lettuce, washed and diced medium

One cucumber, peeled and diced

Eight radishes, washed and sliced

Eight grape tomatoes, sliced in half

Two hard boiled eggs, peeled and sliced

Four slices of bacon, fried crisp and chopped fine

One tablespoon of sunflower seeds

Two tablespoons of dried cranberries

Eight pitted whole Kalamata olives

Two tablespoons of sliced pepperoncini peppers, patted dry

Two ounces of feta cheese, sliced

Half a cup of shredded cheddar cheese

Salt

Ground cracked pepper

Use a medium-sized bowl. Combine all ingredients in order listed. This is a layered salad. Sprinkle on salt. Add fresh ground cracked pepper. Add whatever salad dressing you prefer. (*I prefer to use a good jar of Greek salad dressing.*)

Tuna Fish Salad

Ingredients:

Two cans of white albacore tuna, drained
Six stalks of celery, diced very small
Two teaspoons of sweet pickle relish
And two hard boiled eggs, peeled and diced fine
One half of a red onion, diced fine
1/3 cup of good mayonnaise
Salt and pepper to taste

Add tuna fish to bowl. Mash fine with fork. Add other ingredients together in bowl and mix well.

MEAT ENTREES

A WAY TO A MAN'S HEART IS
THROUGH HIS STOMACH

The saying is that "There is someone for everyone." Sometimes, it takes choosing the wrong person first and overcoming hardships to find that special someone. When you do, you live happier and healthier. The following story will show you to have faith that God will not let you be lonely or unloved. The meat entrees are the heart of the meal and are consumed by men. It seemed appropriate that a story going to the heart of someone you love would fit with these recipes.

Joseph hailed from South Jersey and went into the Navy at 17. He was sent to an aircraft carrier and stationed in Europe. He had the job of helping to launch the planes from the flight deck. He served in Europe for nine months. After Europe, Joseph went to Jacksonville, Fla. He enjoyed Florida so much that he came back to Florida after his discharge.

In 1986, Joseph married his first wife, Regina. His two children were born in 1987 and 1988, respectively. He was with her for nearly 10 years, but he wasn't happy. They separated after the third year and rekindled the relationship. This separation and return occurred regularly during his marriage until he got a divorce. During this turmoil, Joseph searched for help from God. He explored different religions and churches until he found the 7th Day of Adventist. In this faith, Joseph began volunteering his time. He was asked to teach a class because his son was unruly.

The teacher couldn't control him, so Joseph sat in the room with him.

While teaching classes, another parent asked Joseph if he minded dating someone from another faith. He said that it did not pose a problem. He just wanted someone to love. At the same time, Joseph prayed for guidance, help and love.

"Lord, help me find someone to love me as much as I would love her."

Then, the miracle happened. Sherry introduced Joseph to Mary Buckman. The other parent met Mary at the pool. Joseph started dating Mary and found out they had a lot in common. They liked each other. Their relationship grew. Their love grew, but Joseph and Mary were both skittish about marriage. For Joseph, his first marriage kept him from wanting a second one like that. For Mary, her son, Aryk didn't like Joseph and gave Mary problems about it. However, the Lord won't be denied if He chooses someone especially for you. So, after a few years of dating, Joseph was persuaded to go ahead and ask Mary to marry her.

"I tried to be without her, but I found myself very lonely. So, I knew I had to ask her to marry me," Joseph said.

Before Mary met the love her life, she falsely believed that she wasn't worthy of love. She was overweight all through her life. In her mind, that excessive weight became a hindrance to love from her adoptive parents and her siblings. When she met Joseph, life changed for her. He has always been by her side and showered her with lots of love. He always calls her beautiful and makes her feel special.

After her mom died, she was lonely. She was a mother

to her boys. She worked, but those things didn't remove her loneliness. Her mom died in January. That following May she started going to Bayside Community Church of God, but it was originally Hercules Church of God. The church continued to grow and became part of Bayside Community Church of God because it was a much larger church and could hold a larger congregation.

At the church, Mary was learning about God's love and kindness. Every Wednesday night, Mary went to Bible study. She began to learn about the love of Christ and being a part of a church family. The members of the church were supportive and there for her. She enjoyed being with people who were there to love the Lord. She wanted to meet someone. She was nervous because she had a bad experience in her first marriage. When she got married the first time, it was in July and lasted until September. It was an abusive situation. The first husband wouldn't work or support the family. That made her scared to try again.

Her mother and siblings told her that the marriage wouldn't work. Being overweight caused her problems with her first marriage and all relationships. She believed she couldn't be loved. She never had boyfriends or dates. Even though she wanted to go to her high school prom, she was afraid to ask anyone. When she did ask someone, he said no, which didn't help her self-esteem.

When I was going to Hercules Church of God, she met a friend, and said to her, "Am I ever going to meet someone who is going to love me? I would like someone who I could go with to dinner."

Sherry loves God with her whole heart and soul. She was a part of a group called Women for God. She was an inspiration in Mary's life. Sherry always told Mary that God loves her regardless of what she looks like. Mary had always thought God didn't like her because she was overweight.

Sherry said, "God loves you. He will always be with you and care about you. You have Jesus Christ as your Lord and savior." She told Mary to go home and read Matthew Chapter 7 verses 7 through 9, which she did.

Ask and it will be given to you; seek and you will find; knock and the door will be opened to you. For everyone who asks, receives; the ones who seek, find; and the one who knocks, the door will be opened. Which one of you will hand his son a stone when he asks for a loaf of bread or a snake when he asks for a fish?

She read the passage and thought about it. She prayed to meet someone. At the time, she didn't know any better and asked for God's forgiveness for using a ouija board with her friends who were babysitting Aryk at the time. It spelled out Joe's name. According to the board, Mary would meet a man named Joseph. Sherry also knew a Joseph. And, while Mary prayed to meet someone, Joseph also prayed to meet someone. Sherry introduced them. Mary fell in love with him almost at once, but she didn't think it was going to work because they met on a blind date. She didn't think he would come back for another date because Mary was overweight, but he did. He called her on Sunday. They started seeing each other on a regular basis. He took me out to dinner. He came to be with her and the boys on Fridays. It was an incredible time. Mary had kids, and he had kids.

She was distressed about the situation because when she met his kids, they were going through a lot of problems. They were living with their mother and didn't want another mother figure. They didn't want Joseph to be seeing anyone on a steady basis. It was a difficult time. Mary's sons were not on board with the romance either. Her oldest son was the man of the house. He didn't want another man telling him what to do. Despite the family issues, they continued to see each other and fell in love. He thought Mary was beautiful. Mary knew he was "the one," but she was afraid of another marriage not working. She had given her heart to someone else, and it didn't work. She feared giving her heart to Joseph. They dated for three years.

One weekend, Mary asked if Joseph would babysit her boys. Her job as chef often required her to work on yachts on the weekends. Whenever she had to work on the weekends, she had to pay someone to watch them, but the cost was becoming too expensive. That is why Mary asked Joseph if he would watch her kids on the weekend, but he didn't want to do that because the children always gave him a hard time. As his girlfriend, she could understand that, but as a mother, she wondered that if he couldn't watch her kids on a weekend, what would happen when they got married.

Mary wanted to get married again and have another child. He didn't want any of that. She assumed the relationship wasn't going any farther. Therefore, they broke apart, but on Mary's birthday, July 8, he called her and came to her apartment. He wished her a happy birthday, fixed her broken bed and talked. A month later, he proposed to her. He thought they would get married right away, but Mary wanted a Valentine's Day wedding, which they had. She had a beautiful wedding and enjoyed getting married on Valentine's Day. The drawback about getting married on Valentine's Day is that hotels, restaurants and other venues are always packed and expensive.

In a marriage, the little things matter the most. For example, Joseph stayed with Mary when she had her hip-replacement surgery. He stayed overnight in the room. When Mary had to go to rehabilitation, he would go to work at 6:30 in the morning, come home, make her dinner, bring her to the rehabilitation location, stay with her, come home, and then, repeat that process six days a week. He was always there for Mary. When Mary needed him to take care of her, he took care of her willingly. Joseph stood by Mary through illnesses, surgeries, trauma and heart-breaking decisions. He has shown her love that she missed from her previous relationships.

Because her husband is loving, caring and special, Mary knows that God gave her this gift. It was the greatest gift He could have given her.

"I know it was the Lord. I love my husband so much. He showed me that I could be loved and am worth loving. I praise God every day and thank Him for my husband," Mary said.

Mary and Joseph's love story proves that putting faith in God's plan leads to a successful marriage. They have been married for 20 years.

(Meat: the flesh of an animal.)

Aunt Ruth's Meatballs

Ingredients:

Two pounds hamburger meat

Two teaspoons of Worcestershire sauce

One package onion soup mix

One can condensed milk

Four cups of ketchup

¾ cup brown sugar

Mix together first four ingredients and form meatballs. Bake in a 350-degree preheated oven for 30 minutes. Mix together last two ingredients. Mix with meatballs in crock pot. Turn crock pot on high. When hot, turn down to low heat. Then, serve when heated through the meat.

Baby Back Pork Ribs

Ingredients:

Six 1-pound racks of baby back ribs

Two large onions, diced large

One tablespoon of salt

Half a tablespoon of black pepper corn

Two bay leaves

Eight garlic cloves

Two quarts of water

One jar of barbecue sauce

Lay pork standing on edge in a six-quart crock pot. Add two quarts of water. Add garlic, salt, pepper, bay leaves and onions. Cover with lid. Set temperature to high. Cook for about four hours until tender. When you can bend them, they're done. Remove ribs. Place on half baking sheet. Cover with barbecue sauce. Place on broiler until they are nice and bubbly. Enjoy.

Bacon-Wrapped *Filet Mignon*

Ingredients:

Filet mignon

Salt and pepper to taste

One slice partially fried but still soft bacon per *filet*

Olive oil

In a heavy cast-iron pan, add oil and let heat. Fry bacon so it is soft. Put bacon around edges of *filet*. Use toothpick to hold in place. Season with salt and pepper on the ends. Add *filets* to pan. Cook until you get a crust on both sides. Place meat in pan. Preheat oven to 425 degrees. Cook in oven until the desired internal temperature. 135 will be rare; 145

is medium; 155 is medium-well; and 160 is well-done.

Chicken *Cacciatore*

Ingredients:

Three-quarters of a cup of olive oil

A whole chicken cut up into eight pieces, excluding the back and gizzards

A cup and a half of flour

Salt and pepper to taste

One large yellow onion, diced fine

One large green pepper, diced fine

One large red pepper, diced fine

Four stalks of celery, diced fine

One pound of button mushrooms, sliced

One can of diced tomatoes

Two cups of chicken broth

Six garlic cloves, minced fine

Teaspoon oregano

One teaspoon of basil

One teaspoon of thyme

Add oil to six-quart Dutch oven and heat to medium-high. Pat chicken dry with paper towel. Mix flour, salt and pepper to taste. Run chicken through the mixture, shaking off excess. Cook in batches of four pieces at a time. Cook until brown. Remove to paper towel-lined plate. Turn oven down to medium temperature. Add celery, peppers, onions, salt and pepper to drippings. In pot, make sure vegetables are all sweated and cooked. Add garlic and mushrooms. Cook mushrooms down. Once mushrooms are soft, add tomatoes, chicken broth, salt, pepper and spices. Bring to a simmer. Add chicken. Place in a 375-degree preheated oven for one hour. Remove from oven. (*Recipe goes good with any kind of pasta.*)

Chicken *Cordon Bleu*

Ingredients:

Six chicken breasts

Six medium-to-thick slices of black forest deli ham

Six medium-to-thick slices of Swiss cheese

Half a cup of olive oil

Two large cans of mushroom slices

Two chicken gravy packages

Salt and pepper to taste

A cup of whole wheat flour

Half a cup of olive oil

Two cups of water

Quarter cup of toasted slivered almonds

Pat dry chicken breast with paper towel. Cut chicken

breast with boning knife until almost in half. Think about cutting open a roll when doing the chicken. Fold ham in half around cheese. Place between both halves of chicken breast. Add salt and pepper to taste. Add to whole wheat flour, shaking off excess flour. Lay breast top side down in medium-sized deep saute pan. Pour olive oil in pan. Brown both sides golden brown. Remove from pan. Lay on plate. Drain cans of mushrooms. Add mushrooms to saute pan. Use the drippings from the bottom of the pan and cook for five minutes. Add packaged gravy. Add two cups of cold water. Whisk until smooth. Arrange chicken breast in pan with mushroom gravy. Cover with lid. Place in a 350-degree preheated oven. Cook for 30 to 35 minutes. Remove and sprinkle almonds on top. Enjoy.

Chicken *Scallopini*

Ingredients:

Three-quarters of a cup of olive oil

Four chicken cutlets, pounded thin

One and a half cups of flour

Four large eggs

Panko bread crumbs

Salt and pepper to taste

Pound of softened salted butter

One cup of chopped toasted pecans

One cup of firmly packed brown sugar

Cut each chicken cutlet into six even-sized pieces. Whisk eggs lightly. Add to a dish. Mix flour, salt and pepper together. Put into another dish. Add bread crumbs into another dish. Put chicken pieces in flour mixture, shaking off excess. Add to the egg mixture. Add to the bread crumb dish. Take a deep skillet. Add oil on medium-high heat. Put chicken pieces into skillet without crowding them. Cook in batches. Let dry on plate with paper towels on it. In a medium-sized bowl, add softened butter and brown sugar. Mix with hand mixer until light and fluffy. Add pecans and stir together. Pour butter mixture into medium-sized saucepan. Melt mixture until slightly bubbly. Put chicken on a platter. Pour melted butter over chicken and serve.

Chicken Wings

Ingredients:

24 chicken wings

Four cups of flour

Quarter cup of cornstarch

Six large eggs

Salt and pepper for taste

Large bottle of hot sauce

One pound of salted butter

Peanut oil to fill six-quart Dutch oven halfway

Mix two cups of flour, cornstarch, salt and pepper for taste. Pat dry the wings run them through the flour mixture. Place them on a rack to dry. Add peanut oil to Dutch oven and heat to 360 degrees. Cook a few at a time. Add wings into hot oil, not overcrowding the pan. Turn frequently until brown and crispy. Place wings on paper towel-covered plate. Let wings drain. Add one pound of salted butter into a saucepan. Add hot sauce to taste. Take medium-sized bowl and add wings with butter and hot sauce mixture. Toss together. Place on platter with blue cheese and ranch dressings, celery and carrot sticks.

Lemon Chicken

Ingredients:

Five-pound whole chicken

Two lemons

Salt and pepper to taste

Two sticks of softened butter

One small onion, cut into quarters

One garlic ball

Half a cup of olive oil

One pound of carrots, peeled and cut in large chunks

Four potatoes, peeled and cut in large chunks

Zest the lemons into the butter. Add salt and pepper. Pat chicken dry including cavities. Rub chicken with mixture. Place on rack in a roaster. Cut what remains of lemons into quarters and add to cavity. Slice garlic ball into half. Put both halves into cavity. In a medium-sized bowl, add onions, carrots and potatoes. Season with salt and pepper. Add oil. Mix to coat chicken. Arrange vegetables around chicken. Place in 375-degree preheated oven. Cook until the internal temperature of the chicken reaches 160 degrees. Remove chicken from pan. Cover chicken with foil and let rest 15 to 20 minutes before serving. Toss vegetables in remaining chicken drippings. Cut chicken. Remove lemons and garlic from cavity. Serve with vegetables.

Lois's Quick Meal

Ingredients:

One pound of ground chuck

One can of kidney beans

One can of green beans

One can of cream of mushroom soup

Salt and pepper to taste

Brown the ground chuck in a skillet. Drain all the juices. Add cream of mushroom soup. Gently stir. Add the kidney beans and green beans. Season with salt and pepper. Turn down temperature to a low simmer. Stir occasionally for 20 minutes. Serve over mashed potatoes, noodles, pasta or rice. It is delicious.

Louise's Beef Stroganoff

Ingredients:

One pound of stewing beef, cut in half

One medium onion, chopped

One cup sour cream

Half cup red wine

Salt and pepper to taste

Worcestershire sauce to taste

Noodles, cooked according to package

Saute beef with onion in skillet until brown. Add wine and simmer for five minutes. Add Worcestershire sauce. Continue simmering. Add remaining ingredients, except noodles. Stir occasionally to avoid sticking. Turn off heat. Pour sauce over noodles and serve.

Louise's Corned Beef Brisket

Ingredients:

Two- or three-pound corned beef brisket

Seasoned meat tenderizer

Salt and pepper to taste

Two cups of water

Beef bouillon cubes

Dash of basil

One tablespoon of Worcestershire sauce

Pinch of rosemary

Potatoes and carrots, sliced

Three tablespoons flour

One onion, sliced.

Poke meat with fork. Add meat tenderizer into meat with fork. In a six-quart pot, brown meat. Drain excess fat. Season with salt and pepper. While meat is browning, boil water and add bouillon cubes. Add basil, rosemary and Worcestershire sauce. Simmer until bouillon cubes are dissolved. After meat is browned, add mixture to pot with meat. Add onion. Cook for two or three hours until beef is fork-tender. With one hour left to cook, add potatoes and carrots. During the cooking, add extra water when necessary. When done, remove vegetables and beef and place in serving dishes. In the pot, add flour to the meat juices. Stir until desired thickness, adding water if necessary. Pour over meat or serve in small gravy boat or pitcher.

Louise's Irish Casserole

Ingredients:

Six cups shredded cabbage

One onion, sliced

Half pound bacon or ham cubes

Two tablespoons parsley

3/4 cup chicken broth

Salt and pepper to taste

One pound of potatoes, sliced

Two ounces of shredded cheddar

Preheat oven to 350 degrees. Spray a three-quart casserole dish with cooking spray. Layer with cabbage, meat, seasonings, potatoes and cheese. Repeat layers. Pour in chicken broth. Bake in oven for 45 minutes covered. Remove lid and back for another 15 minutes.

Marinated Steaks

Ingredients:

Sirloin steaks, ribeye or New York's porterhouse

¾ cup of olive oil

½ cup of red wine vinegar

A tablespoon of salt

Half a tablespoon of pepper

Four garlic cloves minced

¼ cup of Worcestershire sauce

¼ cup of soy sauce

Place all these ingredients into a large Ziploc bag along with steaks. Toss the bag, working all the sauce into the steak. Place in refrigerator for at least two hours. Remove steaks from bag and pat dry. Grill, fry or bake them.

Meatloaf

Ingredients:

Two pounds of ground chuck

One cup of ketchup

One sweet vidalia onion grated

Four slices of whole wheat bread

Four garlic cloves, minced

Salt and pepper to taste

One teaspoon of basil

One teaspoon of oregano

One teaspoon of thyme

Three-quarters of a cup of milk

Two large eggs

One quarter cup of chopped fresh parsley

1/2 cup of light brown sugar

One tablespoon of Worcestershire sauce

Four slices of uncooked bacon

Add ground beef to a medium-sized bowl. Crack eggs on top of ground beef. Lay bread over top. Pour milk over bread. Let stand for five minutes. Add seasonings, garlic, half of the ketchup, parsley and Worcestershire sauce. Mix with clean hands. Put mixture in a 13 by 9 baking dish and form an oblong loaf. Mix remaining ketchup with brown sugar in a small bowl. Spoon ketchup mixture over top of meatloaf. Lay bacon over top of meatloaf. Insert in preheated oven at 375 degrees. Cook between 45 minutes to one hour until fully cooked.

Mom's Meatballs

Ingredients:

Two pounds of ground chuck

Two small cans of tomato sauce

Half a cup of ketchup

Four slices of whole wheat bread

Salt and pepper to taste

A teaspoon of basil

A teaspoon of oregano

A teaspoon of thyme

Fourgarlic cloves minced

Half cup of chopped parsley

One large sweet vidalia onion grated

Three-quarters of a cup of milk

Two large eggs

Half a cup of olive oil

One tablespoon of Worcestershire sauce

Two and ¾ cups of milk

Two tablespoons of salted butter

One and half cups of flour

1/4 cup of flour

Mix salt and pepper with one and half cups of flour on a plate. In a medium-sized bowl, place the beef. Crack the eggs over top the beef. Add the bread on top. Pour ¾ cup of milk over top of the bread. Let stand for five minutes. Add onion, parsley, spices, garlic and Worcestershire sauce. Add salt, pepper and ketchup. Mix with clean hands. Form into meatballs. Run meatballs through flour mix, shaking off excess flour. Use a deep-sided skillet. Add oil. Heat to medium heat. Add meatballs in single layer. Brown all sides. Once they're browned, add two cans of tomato sauce. Turn down to a low simmer. Cook until meatballs are thoroughly done (about an hour). Remove meatballs leaving sauce and scraps. Add a quarter cup of flour to sauce. Whisk until blended. Add two cups of milk. Whisk together until smooth. Once mixture is thickened, add butter to the sauce. Stir. Pour sauce over meatballs and enjoy. Serve with pasta.

Mom's Pork Roast

Ingredients:

Four pounds of pork roast

One jar of sauerkraut, drained

Six medium potatoes, peeled and diced medium

Two pounds of carrots, peeled and cut large

Half cup of olive oil

Salt and pepper to taste

Six garlic cloves

One large vidalia sweet onion, diced small

Half a cup of olive oil

Pat roast dry with paper towel. Add salt and pepper on all sides of the roast. Pour olive oil over roast. Cook in six quart Dutch oven on medium heat. Brown all sides. Remove roast and put it on a plate. Add onions, carrots, potatoes, more salt and pepper. Stir and let cook to sweat. Try to get a little color on the carrots and potatoes. Turn off heat. Add garlic cloves. Roast on top of everything. Put sauerkraut on top of roast. Place lid on pot. Place in 325-degree preheated oven. Cook for one and half hours. It's done when it is fork-tender. Could take up to two hours. Internal temperature should be 160 to 170 degrees.

Mom's Slow Cooker Roast Beef

Ingredients:

Five pounds of chuck roast

Half a cup of olive oil

Salt and pepper to taste

Four cloves of minced garlic

Two large sweet onions, diced large

Four large potatoes, peeled and diced large

One cup of beef broth

Ketchup

Two pounds of carrots, peeled and sliced in large chunks

Pat dry the chuck roast. Cover the roast entirely with olive oil. Place in a very large saute pan. Brown both sides until crispy. Add carrots to bottom of a crock pot. Shake salt and pepper on them. Place onions on top of that, followed by potatoes. Season with more salt and pepper, followed by garlic cloves. Add beef broth over vegetables. Place the roast on top of the ingredients. Add enough ketchup to cover entire top of roast. Cover with lid. Cook on high for about four to five hours until meat falls apart from the bone and is tender. Serve and enjoy.

Pork Chops

Ingredients:

Four center-cut pork chops, cut to one-inch thick, including tenderloin

Half a cup of olive oil

Salt and pepper to taste

Quarter cup of flour

Two cups of milk

Water

In a large saute pan on medium heat, add olive oil, salt, pepper and pork chops. Brown on both sides to crispy. Add enough water to fill pan halfway. Adjust temperature to medium high. Place lid to cover. Make it loose so steam can escape once water has evaporated. Continue to brown pork chops in remaining drippings. Remove pork chops and add to plate. Reduce heat to medium-low. Add flour, stirring until smooth. Gently whisk in two cups of milk. Add salt and pepper to taste. Pour gravy over pork chops. It is delicious.

Prime Rib of Beef

(*Works for any size prime rib*)

Ingredients:

Prime Rib

One pound and half of softened butter

Salt and pepper to taste

Six to 10 garlic cloves

Two tablespoons of herbs of Provence

Pat the prime rib dry. Take a boning knife. Go into the flesh all the way around the bone. Make holes for pockets. Stuff as many garlic cloves as you wish into the pockets. Add as much salt and pepper as you'd like into the butter. Rub butter all over the prime rib. You want the butter thick on the beef. Place prime rib in a roasting pan. Preheat oven to 450 degrees. Place beef in oven for about 45 minutes. This will get the crust to form. Turn temperature down to 350 degrees and continue to cook until inside temperature reaches desired temperature. Make sure you use your meat thermometer in the center of the roast. 135 will be rare; 145 is medium; 155 is medium-well; and 160 is well-done. Both the ends will be done more than the center. Personally, I wouldn't go above 145 because when you're done, you're going to rest the roast. Resting the roast will raise the temperature more.) Rest it for at least a half hour. When finished, remove the chime bone and carve it. (Save the bone to make soups later.)

Shepherd's Pie

Ingredients:

Two pounds of ground chuck

Small frozen bag of crinkle cut-sliced carrots

Small frozen bag of peas

Six slices of bacon

Three packages of brown gravy mix

One large sweet yellow onion, diced small

Salt and pepper to taste

Eight medium potatoes, peeled and diced medium

Half and half as needed

One stick of salted butter

Six whole garlic cloves

Two cups of shredded cheddar cheese

Take a large deep saute pan. Apply bacon. Brown to crisp. Remove bacon. Insert ground beef. Brown completely. Drain juices. Crumble bacon over beef. Add onions. Read directions for making gravy and make it according to package. Incorporate gravy into meat mixture. Add peas, carrots, salt and pepper to taste. Let simmer for five minutes. Set aside. In a large pot, add potatoes and garlic cloves. Cover with water. Add about a tablespoon of salt. Bring water to boil. Cook potatoes until they are tender. Drain excess water. Add salt and pepper to taste. Add half and half. Use potato masher with enough half and half to make potatoes smooth. Use a 9 by 13 baking dish. Spray with cooking spray. Add meat mixture, then potatoes on top. Sprinkle cheese on top of potatoes. Place in preheated oven of 375 degrees for 30 to 40 minutes until brown and bubbly. Enjoy.

SEAFOOD ENTREES

SEAFOOD, GOD'S WORD GIVES HOPE TO THE DESPAIRED

Throughout life, families struggle. They fight with each other. They struggle financially. They fail to get respect from each other. How people deal with those struggles matters. Those people who can find salvation in God's words will find hope in a hopeless situation. They will survive their traumas. When they look to God, they are happy. They love each other without conditions. They love their children despite their issues. they feel God's presence in their lives. Although having hope when all seems lost is hard to do, God is always there to support us. Opening a Bible will help us remember His love for us. this chapter is dedicated to the Word of God because fish has always been a symbol of Christianity. Seafood is a part of many Christian faiths and shows that God is a part of our lives every day.

If I speak in human and angelic tongues, but do not have love, I am a resounding gong or a clashing cymbal. And if I have the gift of prophesy and comprehend all mysteries and all knowledge, if I have all faith so as to move mountains, but do not have love, I am nothing. If I give away everything I own and if I hand my body over so that I may boast, but do not have love, I gain nothing.

Love is patient. Love is kind. It is not jealous. Love is not pompous. It is not inflated. It is not rude. It does not seek its own interests. It is not quick-tempered. It does not brood over injury. It does not rejoice over wrongdoing but rejoices with the truth. It bears all things, believes all things, hopes all things and endures all things.

Love never fails. If there are prophecies, they will be brought to nothing. If tongues, they will cease. If knowledge, it will be brought to nothing. For we know partially and we prophecy partially, but when the perfect comes, the partial will pass away. When I was a child, I used to talk as a child, think as a child, reason as a child. When I became a man, I put aside childish things. At present, we see indistinctly as in a mirror, but then face to face. At present, I know partially. Then, I shall know fully as I am fully known. So faith, hope and love remain; these three, but the greatest of these is love.

Joseph is supportive of Mary, and she supports him. They both love the Lord with all their hearts. When the Lord is the biggest part of a relationship, a marriage will be and remain strong. They have put God in the center of their marriage. Even though they have seen marriages without God, they doubt they will succeed. People who don't put God at the center of their marriage aren't always happy.

Throughout their lives, they have prayed about their problems. They have faith that God will heal the family in His time. They read passages from Psalms, Solomon and Corinthians and believe that His love is perfect.

At night, Mary thinks about her life. By a coincidence, Mary, her sister and one of Joseph's children bought the same bed in style and brand name. Therefore, when Mary sleeps on her bed, she believes she is connected to the others. It becomes a way to find comfort and solace that reaches across the miles and family strife. It has been a blessing to her to know that all are lying on the same bed. The fact that Joseph is lying next to Mary increases the comforting feeling and solace.

During these times of closeness at night and

throughout the day, Mary thinks about King Solomon and the Psalms. She considered them to be similar to King Solomon and the Queen of Sheba. Their love was intense and beautiful. Like them, Mary and Joseph have endured through problems and joys. When problems arose, the Word of God helped them feel hope and support.

The people we meet throughout our lives often are spreading God's message without realizing it. For example, when Mary went on a big family vacation, she met a woman who used to be the head housekeeper at Trump Tower. Mary had wanted to stay in a Trump hotel. During the conversation she had with the woman, Mary asked what it was like to work for President Trump. She said she enjoyed working for him. When the hotel was busy, Trump would help change the beds and help them in other ways that was needed. He was not afraid of working hard along side the employees. He also was nice to employees and knew everyone by their first name. President Trump made an impact on this woman. Her story made an impact on Mary's life even though it was a brief encounter. She met others throughout her life that impacted her decisions or life.

(Seafood: any form of sea life regarded as food by humans. Seafood prominently includes fish and shellfish.)

Crab Bake Potatoes

Ingredients:

Four large russet potatoes

3/4 of cup of sour cream

16 ounces of shredded cheddar cheese

One tablespoon of freeze-dried chives

Six slices of bacon, fried and chopped

One cup of melted salted butter

Two tablespoons of fresh lemon juice

One pound of lump crab meat

Half a cup of heavy cream

Preheat oven to 425 degrees. After washing, place potatoes in the oven for about an hour and a half until soft to the touch. Remove potatoes. Let them rest until cold enough to touch. Cut them in half. Scoop from skin. Place in a medium-sized mixing bowl. Lay skin from potatoes on a half baking sheet. To the potatoes, add butter, salt and pepper. Add to heavy cream. Stir until blended. Add bacon, sour cream, chives, half of cheese, lemon juice and crab meat. Stir everything together. Add ingredients to the potato skin shells. Add remaining cheese on top. Bake for 20 minutes until cheese is bubbly. It's best to serve with a nice green salad. Enjoy.

Fried Shrimp

Ingredients:

One and a half cups of vegetable oil

One pound of large shelled and deveined shrimp

One and a half cups of flour

Four eggs, whisked

Two cups of Panko bread crumbs

Salt and pepper to taste

One cup of ketchup

Juice from two lemons

Two tablespoons of prepared horseradish

Pat shrimp dry with paper towels. Mix flour with salt and pepper. Add shrimp to flour mixture. Run shrimp through eggs, then bread crumbs. Lay on plate. Add vegetable oil to large saute pan. Add shrimp carefully to pan. Brown on both sides. Remove. Put shrimp on paper towel-lined plate. Sprinkle with salt. In a small mixing bowl, add ketchup, lemon juice and horseradish. Stir to combine. Serve with fried shrimp.

Lemon-Butter Fried Scallops

Ingredients:

One pound of large sea scallops

Quarter cup of fresh lemon juice

Six cloves of minced garlic

Half cup of very good dry white wine

One tablespoon of chopped fresh parsley

Lemon wedges to garnish

One stick of salted butter

Salt and pepper to taste

In a medium-sized skillet, melt butter on medium high. Pat dry scallops. Add salt and pepper to each side. Add scallops to skillet. Sear to golden brown on both sides. Remove scallops. Place on plate. Remove saute pan from heat. Add wine to the pan. Add garlic. Return to heat. Cook until butter is reduced by 1/3. Add lemon juice, parsley, salt and pepper. Add scallops. Heat to warm through the scallops. It is delicious.

Louise's Deviled Crab

Ingredients:

1/4 cup of butter

Half cup of flour

One cup of milk

One pound of lump crabmeat or backfin

One teaspoon of Worcestershire sauce

One teaspoon of chopped parsley

Salt and pepper to taste

Bread crumbs

Melt butter. Add flour. Stir until blended. Add milk, parsley, salt and pepper. Stir until sauce thickens like pudding. Add crab meat. Fold into milk mixture so crab meat doesn't break into pieces. Put into refrigerator to chill. Make either crab cakes or put into casserole dish with bread crumbs on top. Saute crab cakes lightly. Bake casserole in a preheated 350-degree oven for 20 minutes.

Pan-Fried Cod

Ingredients:

Four eight-ounce pieces of cod

Half a cup of olive oil

A cup and a half of flour

Salt and pepper to taste

Four large eggs, whisked together

Fine butter cracker crumbs

Lemon wedges for garnish

Three-quarters of a cup of good mayonnaise

Juice from one lemon

One teaspoon of capers

One teaspoon of crushed dill

One teaspoon of Dijon mustard

Six sweet pickles, diced fine

One teaspoon of Worcestershire sauce

Mix flour with salt and pepper. Add flour mixture to dish. Run cod through mixture, then eggs and cracker crumbs. In a large skillet, add olive oil. Heat to medium-high. Add cod to skillet. and brown on both sides. Remove from heat. Add to 375-degree preheated oven for 20 minutes. Remove from oven. Place on a serving platter. Add lemon wedges for garnish on platter. In a small bowl, add mayonnaise, Dijon mustard, dill, sweet pickles, capers, Worcestershire sauce, juice from one lemon, salt and pepper. Stir to combine. Serve with cod.

Pan-Fried Grouper

Ingredients:

Four eight- to 10-ounce fillets of grouper

A cup and a half of whole wheat flour

Salt and pepper

Juice from two lemons

Eight tablespoons of butter

Add salt and pepper to flour. Add fish to the flour mixture, shaking off excess. Add fish to a large skillet at medium-high temperature with skinned side facing. Brown both sides. Remove from heat. Add two pads of butter per fish. Sprinkle on lemon juice. Place in preheated 375-degree oven. Bake for approximately 15 to 20 minutes until fish is firm to touch. (*This is delicious on a toasted hoagie roll with tartar sauce.*)

Pan-Seared Dover Sole

Ingredients:

Four eight-ounce Dover sole fillets, skinned

Three-quarters of a cup of melted salted butter

Quarter of a cup of olive oil

Salt and pepper to taste

Juice from two lemons

Fresh chopped parsley for garnishing

Take a large saute pan. Add olive oil and butter. Bring to medium-high temperature. Add Dover sole face side down. Brown both sides. Add lemon juice. Add to preheated oven at 425 degrees. Let cook until firm and flaky, about five to 10 minutes. Remove from oven. Garnish with parsley.

Salmon With Ginger Lemon Butter

Ingredients:

Four eight-to 10-ounce center-cut skinned salmon

Half a cup of olive oil

One cup of whole wheat flour

Salt and pepper to taste

One stick of salted butter

One tablespoon of ground fresh ginger

Two lemons, cut in half

Add flour to a plate with salt and pepper. Mix together. Take a large saute pan. Add olive oil. Bring to medium heat. Lay salmon in pan skin side facing. Brown both sides. Add salt to pan. Place salmon in preheated 375-degree oven for five to 10 minutes. When you start to see the white fat or protein surface, it's done. Remove from oven. Let rest. In a small sauce pan, melt butter. Squeeze lemon halves over butter. Add ginger. Heat thoroughly. Place salmon on serving platter. Pour melted butter over salmon. (*This goes good with cooked jasmine rice.*)

Shrimp *Fettuccine Alfredo*

One pound of large shrimp peeled and deveined

Skewers as needed soaked in water for at least two hours

Half a cup of fresh lemon juice

Quarter cup of good olive oil

Six minced garlic cloves

Salt and pepper to taste

One pound of *fettuccine* noodles

Two cups of heavy whipping cream

Two cups of freshly grated Parmesan cheese

Two sticks of salted butter

Eight garlic cloves

Fresh cracked black pepper

Two tablespoons finely chopped fresh parsley

In a medium-sized bowl, add shrimp, oil, lemon juice, salt and pepper. Add garlic cloves. Stir. Cover with plastic wrap. Let marinate in fridge for at least two hours. After two hours, remove shrimp. Place six shrimp on each skewer. In a large pot, add four quarts of water with salt. Bring to boiling. Heat a grill pan to medium-high heat. Cook fettuccine noodles in boiling water per package instructions. In a medium-sized saucepan, add butter, salt, pepper and garlic. Sauteed garlic and butter for a few minutes. Add heavy whipping cream. Turn down to medium low. While whisking, add Parmesan cheese. Get the ingredients warmed and mix. It will burn if it boils. Once thickened remove from Heat. Drain pasta in a colander and pour into large pasta bowl. Add creamed mixture and toss. Sprinkle on second cup of Parmesan cheese and parsley. Add cracked pepper. Take skewered shrimp. Add to medium-sized grill pan for a minute and a half on each side at medium-high on top of stove. Remove skewers. Add pasta to individual serving bowls with a couple of skewers of shrimp on top. Add fresh cracked pepper. (*This is my kids' favorite.*)

Shrimp Scampi

Ingredients:

Six garlic cloves, minced

One teaspoon of salt

Six tablespoons of olive oil, divided in half

One pound of large shrimp, peeled and deveined

Half a teaspoon of red pepper flakes

Half a cup of chicken broth

Two tablespoons of fresh lemon juice

One stick of softened salted butter

Two tablespoons of chopped parsley

One French baguette

In a medium-sized bowl, add garlic, salt and half the olive oil. Add shrimp. Toss to coat. Chill uncovered for at least one hour. Add remaining oil to a large skillet over medium heat. Add to shrimp mixture. Make sure not to burn the garlic. Shrimp should be pink and slightly underdone about a minute-and-a-half. Transfer shrimp to plate with a slotted spoon. Keep as much oil in skillet as possible. Add red pepper to skillet. Toss until fragrant, about one minute. Add chicken broth and lemon juice. Cook, stirring occasionally. Reduce temperature by half. Add butter and cook until butter is soft and sauce has thickened. Add shrimp and juices for shrimp into skillet. Cook for two minutes. Add parsley. Slice *baguette.* Serve along side shrimp dipping *baguette* into sauce.

Trout

Ingredients:

Four cleaned trout

One stick of butter, softened

Salt and pepper to taste

One teaspoon of paprika

Juice from two lemons

Mix butter with salt and pepper. Lay trout onto 1/2 baking sheet pan sprayed with cooking spray. Brush with softened butter. Sprinkle on paprika. Place in the oven set to broiler. Watch carefully until fish gets brown, bubbly and firm. Remove from oven. Pour on lemon juice. Enjoy.

EGG DISHES

ENJOY MIRACLE OF LIFE
WITH EGG DISHES

The reason eggs are used during Easter and Passover is because they represent new life. Spring is the season for new life. Flowers are blooming. Trees have buds on them. Animals mate and have babies. Therefore, stories about births fit most appropriately with the egg dishes. Although all children are gifts from God, they aren't always easy to manage. They aren't always easy deliveries. As they grow, they give us challenges that often stretch our patience. They test the limits of our love, but eventually, the blessings of children are known. Joseph and Mary had struggles like all parents, but some of their struggles go beyond what all parents experience. That made them appreciate their children and love them more. As you read their story, think about how you are tested with your children.

After Joseph and Mary got married, they lived in Clearwater, Fla., Mary's son, Aryk, became uncontrollable. When Aryk went into the facility, Mary was pregnant with Solomon.

During her pregnancy, Mary worked at Bon Appetite. At 26 weeks pregnant, she moved from the kitchen to the office to sell gift certificates. At 37 weeks pregnant, Mary felt a strong urge to have the baby that day even though she wasn't due for another three weeks. She was expected to go to the restaurant's office to sell gift certificates. Instead, she saw her doctor and was told she was showing no signs that she had started labor. She wasn't dilated, but her strong sense kept telling her she had to have the baby. She went to the hospital to have an ultrasound and to see the midwife.

The ultrasound showed nothing was wrong either, but at Mary's request, the midwife spoke with Dr. Dawson who admitted Mary and induced labor.

Solomon came into the world the next morning at 5:30 a.m. When he was born, he didn't cry and was blue. They rushed him to the neonatal infant care unit. The workers took blood samples and ran tests. According to the hospital, Solomon had a bowel infection. He was transferred to All Children's Hospital by an ambulance. The doctor at All Children's Hospital told Mary that if she had waited for the three weeks or for when the baby wanted to be born naturally, Solomon would have been stillborn. The bowel infection would have killed him *in utero*. While at All Children's Hospital, the baby needed blood transfusions. The blessing of the birth was marred by the uncertainty of the baby's health.

Joseph and Mary stayed at Ronald McDonald House. Ryan stayed with friends from church, but he got sick with asthma. Aryk was in the residential facility, but during this time, the residential facility decided Aryk needed to be released. Mary was dealing with a baby in the NICU at All Children's Hospital; Ryan was on the third floor of All Children's with asthma; and Aryk was recently released from a residential facility. Despite the trying times, Joseph, Mary, Solomon, Aryk and Ryan made it through the ordeal.

The joy came when Joseph and Mary could bring home little Solomon. He came home on their first anniversary, Mary's present to Joseph. Today, Solomon is a healthy 19-year-old. However, as he was growing, Mary feared that Solomon might be too sickly. Doctors recommended that he not go into day care, which meant Mary had to be a full-time mom. She was concerned for his health throughout his life and was frequently calling her favorite doctor for help.

Before Solomon was born, Joseph fought for custody of his two children from his first marriage. He finally got custody of his two children around the time of Solomon's birth. Mary and Joseph were living with four teenagers and a newborn baby in an apartment. They needed more space. A real estate agent helped them find a new house for the family. He brought her to what the agent called, "the perfect house" for them. Mary thought the house was ugly. However, she decided it just needed someone to take care of it and love it. Mary and Joseph bought it and have been fixing it for 19 years. Now, it feels like home. They raised all five kids in that house. Time passed, and the children wanted to go their different paths. At age 17, one of Joseph's children took Joseph to court to be emancipated. Her mother got custody of the child. Mary feared that the child would have problems and was correct. The child quit counseling and school. She became pregnant at 17. Joseph's other child decided to live with the first one.

Children represent new life and blessings like egg dishes in this cookbook. However, raising children is never easy but is always fulfilling.

(Eggs: a food product produce from poultry that is used as both an ingredient or a main dish. Eggs can be cooked by boiling, poaching, frying, microwaving and baking. They are one of the most common ingredients for food preparation.)

Classic French *Omelet*

Ingredients:

Two large eggs

Two tablespoons of half and half

Salt and pepper to taste

One tablespoon of butter

Half cup of pork, cheese, potatoes, beef or onions

Make sure everything is cooked except cheese before adding. In a small bowl, mix eggs, salt, pepper and half-and-half. Whisk. Heat butter in a medium-sized nonstick skillet or *omelette* pan at medium high. Add eggs. Completely fill the bottom of the skillet. Tilt pan to get it to cook evenly across the whole bottom. With a rubber spatula, start moving the eggs from the outside edge into the center. This would move the eggs from the center to the outside edge. Cook all eggs but softly. Add skillet to the broiler beforehand. Add the ingredients on top. Finish with cheese. Once cheese is melted and bubbly, remove from oven. Fold in half. Serve on plate immediately. (*Have fun with this. Sometimes, add leftovers. Use different cheeses. Garnish*

with sour cream and caviar. Add guacamole or salsa.
Make every omelet your own.)

Deviled Eggs

Ingredients:

12 hard boiled eggs, peeled

Three-quarters of cup of good mayonnaise

Salt and pepper to taste

One tablespoon of yellow mustard

One teaspoon of sugar

One teaspoon of red wine vinegar

Paprika

12 pitted Kalamata olives, patted dry and cut in half

Slice eggs in half lengthwise. Remove yolks. Add yolks to mixing bowl. Add mayonnaise, mustard, red wine vinegar, sugar, salt and pepper. Mix all ingredients together until smooth. (*I like to add the mixture into a star tipped piping bag.*) Spoon it back into egg halves. Sprinkle with paprika. Add half an olive to each egg if desired. Garnish with cooked shrimp or caviar.

Eggs and Bacon Salad

Ingredients:

Eight hard-boiled eggs

Eight slices of bacon cooked crisp, then chopped

Three-quarters of a cup of good mayonnaise

One tablespoon of mustard

One teaspoon of red wine vinegar

One teaspoon of sugar

Salt and pepper to taste

Grate hard boiled eggs on box grater. Add to a medium-sized mixing bowl. Add bacon, salt, pepper, mayonnaise, mustard, red wine vinegar and sugar. Stir. Make sandwiches or dip with it. If used as dip, use with bagel chips.

Eggs Benedict

Ingredients:

Four English muffins, cut in half

One stick of salted butter, softened

Eight pieces of Canadian bacon

Eight extra large eggs

Four extra large egg yolks

Four tablespoons of freshly squeezed lemon juice

Salt and pepper to taste

A pinch of cayenne pepper

One tablespoon of white vinegar

12 tablespoons of unsalted butter, softened

For Hollandaise Sauce:

Place egg yolks, lemon juice, salt, pepper and cayenne pepper into blender. Turn on low for 15 seconds. Place unsalted butter in a saucepan, heating until sizzling hot. Add butter into blender in a steady, drizzling stream. Continue mixing on low until sauce is very thick. Toast all English muffin halves until brown. Spread immediately with salted butter. Take Canadian bacon. Add to skillet with two tablespoons of butter. Set at medium-high heat. Brown both sides. Remove. Put on plate covered with paper towels. In a large saucepan, fill halfway with water. Add one tablespoon of white vinegar. Bring to boil. Stir with wooden spoon. Stir constantly until whirlpool is created. Crack an egg over the middle of the whirlpool. Cook until egg whites are done and yoke is still running. Remove with a slotted spoon. Place on a plate. Repeat until all eggs are poached. Start building your eggs Benedict. Start with English muffin. Place bacon on top, followed by poached egg. Add Hollandaise sauce. Garnish with sprinkles. (*When cooked right this is my absolute favorite.*)

Eggs Benedict *Florentine*

Use the eggs Benedict recipe but instead of using Canadian bacon use this creamed spinach on the English muffin.

Recipe for the creamed spinach

Ingredients:

Four tablespoons of salted butter
One pound bag of baby spinach
Quarter cup of freshly grated Parmesan cheese
Salt and pepper to taste
Half a cup of half and half

In a nonstick medium-sized skillet, melt butter to hot temperature. Add in baby spinach. Saute with a wooden spoon. Stir until spinach is wilted. Add salt and pepper. Add half and half. Stir. Add Parmesan cheese.

Egg *Frittatas*

Ingredients:

Six eggs
Two tablespoons of butter
A third a cup of milk
Half a teaspoon of herbs: (basil, oregano or thyme)
Rosemary
Herbs of Provence
Salt and pepper to taste

One cup vegetables, blanched

One cup sliced boiled potatoes or frozen hash browns

¾ cup meat

Sliced onions

Shredded cheese

In a medium-sized mixing bowl, add eggs, milk, herbs, salt and pepper. Add vegetables, meat, potatoes and cheese. Add butter to nonstick saute pan. Heat to medium. Once butter is bubbly hot, add in egg mixture. Let cook for about two minutes. Place in 375-degree preheated oven. Bake until set and toothpick inserted comes out clean. Remove. Slice and place on a platter along with sour cream, salsa or guacamole. Delicious.

Jelly *Omelet*

Ingredients:

Same as *omelet*

Half teaspoons of sugar

½ teaspoon of vanilla

Fruit preserves

Mix all ingredients. Put in sugar and vanilla extract before cooking eggs. Cook egg mixture the same as omelet recipe. Add preserves or jellies. Fold in half. Finish with powdered sugar on top.

Louise's Passion for Cheese *Omelet*

Ingredients:

Three slices of white American cheese

Three slices of Provolone cheese

Three eggs

Pepper

1/4 cup Parmesan cheese

Half cup of shredded mozzarella cheese or cheddar

In a bowl, beat eggs with whisk or fork. Beat until eggs are frothy. Tear two slices of American and provolone into pieces. Add torn cheese to bowl with eggs. Beat again lightly. Add parmesan, shredded cheese and pepper. Beat again lightly. Use either an *omelet* maker or frying pan. If you use an *omelet* maker add a tablespoon of butter to each side of the pan. When pan is hot, pour egg mixture into pan. Let cook until brown on bottom and sides. If you are using an *omelet* maker, close lid. If using a pan, flip with spatulata over to one side. Cook one to two minutes more. Place final two slices of cheese on top of eggs. Let melt. Serve.

Mom's French Toast

Ingredients:

Six large eggs

One cup of half and half

One tablespoon of brown sugar

One teaspoon of cinnamon

One teaspoon of vanilla extract

Six slices of thick bread

In a medium-sized mixing bowl, add eggs. Whisk together. Add half and half, vanilla, cinnamon and sugar. In a medium high-temperature griddle, add butter until melted. Add bread into egg mixture. Leave for just a couple of seconds. Place into griddle. Brown both sides until golden brown. Finish with warm maple syrup and butter.

Quiche Lorraine

Ingredients:

One ready-made pie crust for 9-inch pie

Six strips of bacon, fried crispy and crumbled

One onion, diced small

One cup of gruyere, shredded

One cup of dry navy beans

One cup of Swiss cheese cubed

Half a cup of freshly grated Parmesan cheese

Six large eggs, lightly beaten

Two cups of heavy cream

Half a teaspoon of nutmeg

Half a teaspoon of salt

Quarter teaspoon of freshly ground pepper

Tabasco sauce to taste

One tablespoons of salted butter

Preheat oven to 400 degrees. Add pastry to 9-inch pie pan. Remove excess. Crimp edges with fork. Lay down a piece of parchment paper on top of pie crust. Place navy beans on top of parchment paper. Add to oven for 10 to 15 minutes till golden brown. Reduce temp to 375. Remove from oven, discarding beans and parchment paper. Add crumbled bacon to pie crust. Take a medium-sized skillet set to medium-high heat. Add butter. Cook onion to transparent. Place onion on top of bacon. Add cheeses on top. In a medium-sized bowl, mix eggs, cream, nutmeg, salt, pepper and Tabasco sauce. Add egg mixture into pie. Place on baking sheet in oven. Cook until knife when inserted in center of pie comes out clean. When done, remove pie from oven. Rest for 10 minutes. Serve. (*As a side note, you can add cooked meat or cheese.*)

Scrambled Eggs

Ingredients:

Six large eggs

Four tablespoons of butter

Salt and pepper to taste

In a nonstick saute pan, add two tablespoons of butter. Heat. In a small mixing bowl, mix eggs with salt and pepper. Whisk until eggs are frothy. Add eggs to pan, stirring constantly on medium heat. Keep stirring. Add remaining butter. Serve soft, being careful not to make them too hard or too dry. Serve with bacon, sausage and toast.

CHEESE DISHES

PETS AND CHEESE ARE
FAMILY FAVORITES

It is easy to think of animals when thinking about cheese. Dairy products come from farmers who process milk, cheese and butter. If you had a tray of cheese on a coffee table, dogs and cats might steal some pieces. Pets love to eat cheese. Watching them sneak the cheese is entertaining. Kids will help dogs and cats sneak some cheese by providing it for them. Some cheese dishes are the first things kids learn to make and share with pets. Macaroni and cheese is considered a comfort food and family favorite because it is inexpensive to make and loved by children everywhere. While the dishes in this section might be more complicated than straight macaroni and cheese, they are worth knowing and trying. However, make sure you keep your dogs and cats away from the cheese!

When Mary turned eight, she got a French poodle. She named her Fifi Marie, which started her tradition that pets should have a first and middle name. Fifi Marie lived for 10 years. However, she did not do well when Mary and her mother moved from Maryland to Virginia to Florida. The poodle had a bad case of fleas when they moved to Florida. The vet didn't sell topical flea treatments or those gummies that dogs eat today. Mary washed Fifi Marie with flea shampoo and used a flea collar, but the treatments didn't work to alleviate Fifi Marie's problem. The bad case of fleas led to pain for the dog and seizures. At 18, Mary was told that the dog had to be put down because the poodle suffered too much. She felt sad but enjoyed the 10 years with her dog.

Next, Mary got a cat. She was married to her first
husband when they went to the Society for the Prevention
of Cruelty to Animals. Mary didn't keep this cat long.
It became a symbol of her first marriage because the
relationship with the cat lasted as long as the relationship
with the huband. The husband took the cat with him to
Virginia. When Joseph and Mary moved into their house,
Mary said she wanted to get a kitten. Joseph agreed. At the
shelter, she saw this cat shivering in a cat box. She was a
year old. Her hair fell off her body. The shakes and hair were
caused by stress. The poor cat had not been put in a cage
before going to the shelter. The Humane Society told Mary
and Joseph that Sophie was a medically needy cat. Mary fell
in love with her immediately, but the cat picked Joseph as
her favorite. She climbed on Joseph's lap and slept on his
clothes when Joseph went to work. When Joseph traveled
for his job occasionally, Sophie took revenge on him for
leaving by peeing on his side of the bed. The vet told Mary
it was a behavioral issue and not to worry. One morning,
Mary found Sophie dead under the bed. She was 10. Mary
wrapped her in Joseph's work clothes and buried her.

Before Sophie died, Mary and Joseph were shopping
in PetSmart. They heard a five-week-old kitten meowing
and screaming in a cage. It was a Mainecoon. Mary
wanted to take this one home with her. Mary named this
cat Sylvester Joe. He became Mary's special friend. She
nicknamed him Joe-Joe. At age nine, Joe-Joe caught
pneumonia, which kept getting worse. Mary tried injections
because the vet said that injections are sometimes more
effective. However, he didn't get better. He had congestive
heart failure. On New Year's Eve, he died. She cried when
she had to say good-bye to Joe-Joe.

After Sophie died, a friend who worked in the

newborn nursery at Busch Gardens told Mary that an old female tabby was pregnant and about to give birth. The cat gave birth to four kittens who needed to be bottle-fed. Mary volunteered to bottle-feed one of the cats and be a foster mother. She named him Ebony Wolfgang. When the six weeks passed, Mary became attached to Ebony. Therefore, she kept him. Ebony remains alive today at 13.

Besides cats, Mary fell in love with dogs too. Her friend is a chihuahua breeder. When Mary visited the breeder's house, she would let Mary hold the dogs and rock them. Mary wanted one, but the cost was expensive. Then, one day, at a barbecue, Mary, Joseph and the couple that bred the dogs discussed a puppy that was seven weeks old. The breeder couldn't sell her because the puppy's legs were too short. Mary held that puppy throughout the barbecue and was saddened when she had to leave her with the breeders. The breeder's husband worked with Joseph as a contractor. He told Joseph to give Mary the puppy. Joseph brought home the puppy and they named her Lucy Esmerelda after her favorite television character Lucy Ricardo. Ebony loved the puppy. Mary took dog-training classes and brought her dog with her wherever she went. At this time, Joseph wanted a chihuahua of his own. Mary's friends allowed her to make payments instead of all at once. She took home the dog on Joseph's Sept. 16th birthday. His name was Boo-Boo Ricardo after *Yogi Bear* and *I Love Lucy*. At four months old, Mary brought Boo-Boo to the vet to have him neutered, but it was too late. Lucy was already pregnant with puppies. Mary got her house ready for the puppies. She cleaned the house and created a space for her to have the puppies. Lucy had her first puppy, Snowflake Hey, at home, but Mary got nervous and wanted Lucy to have the rest at the vet. Lucy had two more puppies. The last was a girl puppy, who was promised to Mary's friend, Sarah. Her dog had recently died. Sarah named the girl puppy Ester. When Lucy tried to nurse her puppies, she would shake. The vet said Lucy lost too many nutrients during the nursing process. Due to the strain of nursing the puppies, Lucy had something wrong with her heart. The vet could solve the problem with Lucy's heart, but it would cost $1,000 for the treatment. Mary asked Sarah for help. Sarah helped her get Lucy healed, but when Lucy was healed, she was told not to nurse. Therefore, Sarah took Lucy for two weeks while Mary bottle fed the dogs. Ester wasn't eating and needed to be tube-fed, but she died anyway. The doctor gave Ester a 50 percent chance of living. Mary was afraid Ester died because she did something wrong. She had bottle fed her cat who is still alive. The vet told her it wasn't her fault.

Sarah went to a Christian women's retreat where she met another dog breeder. The breeder offered Sarah a white dog who had a litter of puppies. Ethel Mae was given to Mary, but it died quickly like Ester. Mary couldn't understand how she could have lost two puppies. The vet reassured her that sometimes dogs have problems. When the puppies turned six weeks old, she and Joseph discussed what to do with them. Mary thought it would be difficult to find the right person to take the puppies. Thus, she kept them. They are like her children. After Snowflake, Mary has Moose Myam and Spike Brutus who is named for a character in Popeye. All dogs have been spaded, neutered and microchipped. Lucy also had a hernia and other problems that were fixed when she was spaded. They sleep on their beds or near them.

Ryan lived with one of Joseph's kids who bred pitbulls. Ryan asked for a puppy. He called her precious puppy, but he never named the dog. Mary named the puppy Penelope Jo and nicknamed the dog, Jo-Jo, in a tribute to her cat. When Ryan moved to Minnesota, he decided that he couldn't bring Jo-Jo with him. Ryan knows that Mary and Joseph will take care of her. While Ryan had the dog, it helped him with his psychological issues. The pitbull ate part of the couch and the black dining room chairs, but she appears to be over the chewing phase. Mary and Joseph welcomed this new member to the family of six dogs and a cat.

All these animals bring the couple joy, but it breaks Mary's heart when people are cruel.

(Cheese: a dairy product derived from milk that is produced in a wide range of flavors, textures and forms by coagulation of the milk protein casein. It comprises proteins and fats from milk, usually the milk of cows, buffalo goats or sheep.)

Apple-Walnut *Brie* in Puff Pastry

Ingredients:

One sheet of frozen puff pastry thawed

One round *brie* cheese

Two tablespoons of softened salted butter

Pinch of salt

Half a cup of flour to spread on table top and to lightly flour your rolling pin

Two apples, peeled, cored and sliced

Quarter cup of brown sugar

Half a cup of walnuts toasted in the oven

Half teaspoon of ground cinnamon

Lay flour on the table and roll out pastry to flatten. Place cheese in center of pastry. In a small saute pan on medium-high heat, add butter and melt. Add apples. Cook them for a few minutes. Add them to brown sugar. Add walnuts followed by a pinch of salt and cinnamon. Toss together and put in pan. Cook until caramelized and tender. Add mixture on top of cheese. Wrap pastry around cheese and apples like a package. Place on oiled half sheet baking pan. Place in a 375-degree preheated oven. Bake until pastry is golden brown. Remove from oven, transferring onto a platter. Cut into wedges. Serve with bread and crackers.

Blue Cheese Dressing

Ingredients:

Three-quarters of a cup of Greek yogurt, plain

Three-quarters of a cup of sour cream

One cup of blue cheese crumbles

Salt and pepper to taste

One tablespoon of Worcestershire sauce

One teaspoon of onion powder

One teaspoon of red wine vinegar

Two garlic cloves minced

A half a cup of buttermilk

In a medium mixing bowl, add yogurt followed by sour cream and buttermilk. Whisk together. Add Worcestershire sauce, vinegar, garlic, onion powder, salt and pepper. Mix together. Gently fold in the blue cheese crumbles. Refrigerate for at least an hour. (*Goes well with chicken wings or a crudite platter. You also might want to pour over a garden salad.*)

Cheese Ball

Ingredients:

One block of cream cheese, softened to room temperature

One and a half cups of chopped pecans

One cup of shredded white cheddar cheese

Three-quarters of a cup of crumbled blue cheese

One tablespoon of Worcestershire sauce

One and 1/2 tablespoons of grated onion

In a medium-sized mixing bowl, add the cream cheese. Stir with a wooden spoon. Add onion, salt, pepper,Worcestershire sauce and blue cheese. Stir until well-combined. Add white cheddar cheese. Mix well. Form ingredients into a ball. Put pecans on an empty plate. Remove cheese ball from bowl and rub into the pecans. Place in an airtight container. Let chill for at least an hour. Then place on a platter with a variety of crackers. Enjoy.

Cheese Fondue

Ingredients:

Two cups dry white wine

Three-quarters of a pound of shredded Swiss cheese

Three-quarters of a pound of shredded gryere cheese

Four tablespoons of all-purpose flour

Half a teaspoon of salt

Half a teaspoon of nutmeg

In a medium-sized saucepan, put in the wine. Simmer for a few minutes. Add both cheeses to a medium-sized bowl. Toss flour in with the cheeses. Add cheese mixture into wine, stirring constantly. After mixtures are smooth, stir in salt and nutmeg. Pour into fondue pot. Light candle under pot. For garnish, take a French *baguette* and slice into cubes. Dip into cheese fondue. (*Also delicious when served with fresh vegetables, such as broccoli, cauliflower, grape tomatoes, carrots and sugar snap peas. You can serve with cubed ham and chicken.*)

Cheese Sauce

Two cups of milk, divided in half

Eight teaspoons of all purpose flour

Half teaspoon of salt

Three ounces of shredded sharp cheddar cheese

Black pepper to taste

In a small bowl, add one cup of milk and flour. Whisk well. In a medium saucepan, pour milk and flour into it. Stir and add remaining milk and salt. Bring to boil over medium heat. Stir frequently. Reduce heat to low and let simmer for about two minutes until lightly thickens. Stir constantly.

Remove from heat. Stir in cheese and pepper. Keep stirring until cheese melts. (*You can serve this over cooked vegetables broccoli or whatever you desire.*)

Cheese Tray

Ingredients:

Round *Brie*

Hummus or guacamole

Hard cheeses

Sliced cheeses

Age cheeses

Semi-firm cheeses

Gouda cheese

Cream cheese with chives

Sliced ham

Dried pepperoni

Salami

Fruit preserves

Variety of crackers

Grapes, mint and fresh basil for garnish

(*My favorite thing to do is make cheese platters.*) Take a platter. Start in the center with round of *brie*. Add hummus or guacamole. Add hard cheese, sliced cheese, aged cheese and semi-firm cheeses. The cheeses could be made from cow's milk, goat's milk or sheep's milk. Add gouda or cream cheese with chives. After you add the cheese, place sliced ham, dried pepperoni and salami. Add a jar of preserves to the tray. (*My favorite preserve is blackberry.*) Finally, place a variety of crackers around the meat. Garnish with grapes, mint and a cluster of fresh basil.

Cheesies

Ingredients:

Four slices of bread (any kind)

Four slices of cheese (any kind)

Softened salted butter to spread onto bread

Using a half sheet tray, lay the bread on the tray. Butter the tops lightly. Lay a slice of cheese on top. Put it under the broiler until cheese is bubbly. Remove from oven. Place on a plate. (*I used to have this when I was a little. I needed it while walking to school. If you use American cheese the cheese will puff up more.*)

Fried Feta

Ingredients:

One pound block of feta cheese

One and 1/2 cups of all-purpose flour

Salt and pepper to taste

Four large eggs, whisked

Two cups of Panko bread crumbs

One cup of slivered almonds

Two cups of vegetable oil

In a dish, add flour, salt and pepper. Mix together. In another dish, place the eggs. In another dish, the Panko bread crumbs mixed with almonds. Take feta cheese and unwrap. Pat dry with paper towels. Cut feta in half. Then cut it into 3/4 inch strips. Run this through the flour mixture followed by the eggs followed by the bread crumbs mixture. Lay on platter or plate. Add oil to deep-sided saute pan. Adjust temperature in pan until temperature reaches 375 degrees. Add cheese into hot oil. Brown on one side. Very carefully, turn over and brown other side. Remove from pan. Place on platter covered with paper towels. Lightly salt the cheese. It is delicious with fresh or jarred salsa.

Louise's Tuna Cream Cheese Sauce

Ingredients:

One eight-ounce package of cream cheese, softened

Two tablespoons of butter

One cup of milk

One can of tuna

One onion, chopped

One can of green vegetable

Two tablespoons of Parmesan cheese

Salt and pepper to taste

Pasta

Prepare pasta according to package. Melt butter in three-quart pot. Add onion. Cook until almost transparent. Add milk. Stir. Add vegetable with water. Stir. Cut cream cheese into smaller pieces. Add to pot. Cook for 10 minutes and until cream cheese is melted. Add tuna. Break tuna pieces into smaller sizes. Stir constantly to keep from sticking. Cook five minutes. Add Parmesan, salt and pepper. Cook another two minutes. Pour over pasta. (*Leftover sauce makes a great sandwich on toasted bread the next day.*)

Mom's Cream Cheese and Onion Dip

Ingredients:

One eight-ounce package of cream cheese, softened at room temperature

One small sweet vidalia onion, graded

Quarter cup of milk

In a medium-sized mixing bowl, add cream cheese followed by onion. With a wooden spoon, stir until creamy. Add milk. Stir again until smooth. Serve with potato chips. (*This is the best dip I ever had.*)

Pimento Cheese

Ingredients:

One eight-ounce block of cream cheese, softened at room temperature

Two cups of shredded sharp cheddar cheese

One cup of Duke's Mayonnaise

One small jar of pimentos, drained

One garlic clove, minced

Salt and pepper to taste

Quarter teaspoon of cayenne pepper

Add cream cheese to large mixing bowl. Add garlic, salt, pepper and cayenne. Add mayonnaise. Stir with wooden spoon until creamy. Fold in sharp cheddar cheese followed by pimentos. Stir until mixed. Spread on dark pumpernickel bread. (*I like to add ham or luncheon meat.*)

VEGETABLES

GIVE CHILDREN VEGETABLES FOR HEALTHY MEALS, KIDS

When children are born, it is a joyous occasion. As they are being raised, parents always question their methods. They make mistakes and often have problems with them. Some children have physical issues that could be overcome with medicine, doctor visits or diet. Others have mental issues that are harder to combat. The food parents give their children can help alleviate some issues but not all. For example, if your child has an allergy, you know not to give that food to the child. If they are hyperactive, you should cut out sugar, caffeine and food with dyes. Vegetables provide healthy alternatives to those foods that can cause problems. Food also can provide comfort for children when sick and calm them when they are out of control. Sometimes, all parents can do is pray for guidance and love them despite their challenges.

Mary was not in a relationship when she got pregnant with Aryk, her Little Sweet Potato. The man was married and sleeping with Mary before Mary told him to take a hike. He didn't want anything to do with the child Mary carried. This was better for her and her child. She lived in Clearwater, Fla., when he was born.

When Mary was in her seventh month, she began to have contractions. A midwife told her she could delay the labor if she drank beer or wine, but Mary was afraid something would happen to the baby if she did that. At the time, she held a full-time job, but the midwife recommended she quit her job and go on bed rest. She was able to carry Aryk to term. He was born on his due date. She picked the name because when she was in third grade, the teacher announced a new student with this name. She always liked it from that moment.

After Aryk was born, Mary lived on assistance from the government. Her social worker recommended she get day care so she could go to school. At six months old, Mary put Aryk in day care while she attended cooking school. However, Aryk already showed signs that problems were beginning. He wouldn't take naps and was difficult for the day care provider. He needed more structure. Mary's mother opened a day care so that Aryk would have a place to go. When he was in kindergarten, Aryk wasn't behaving in school. None of the schools wanted to take him. He went to counseling services and began going to a special school for behavior issues. His behavior at home wasn't any better than at school. He was hard to handle. The police were called regularly.

Meanwhile, Ryan was born 23 months after Aryk. The father of this one didn't want to be involved with the baby. Mary and her mother, who ran a special needs day care, tried a number of parenting techniques, such as 1-2-3 Magic, but they failed to get Aryk's behavior under control. He wouldn't listen. And, when his anger escalated, his eye color turned from blue to green. Aryk would hit his head on the coffee table regularly, scaring Mary. She would call the police to get him to stop. although she struggled with raising Aryk, she did have some help besides her mother. In-home therapists were able to reach Aryk. John, one therapist, was able to connect with both boys. He would provide activities for the boys. John recommended that Aryk start karate lessons, but Mary had no extra income to cover the lessons or other activities. The money she earned from Bon Appetite barely covered the bills. Her mother also helped her until she got sick. The doctors claimed it was pneumonia, but when a pulmonary doctor examined Mary's mother, he found a cyst that was growing in her lung. The fist-sized cyst was the result of a pea that had landed in her lung. Tissue was growing around the pea. Her mother couldn't do the day care any more. Aryk was nine while Ryan was seven. Later, her mother had to have by-pass surgery due to clogged arteries. The surgeon nicked her heart, and Mary's mother died. Because her mother helped raised Aryk and he saw her more than his mother, Mary's mother's death hit him hard. He didn't know how to deal with it. John helped Aryk, Ryan and Mary through this difficult time. He offered to babysit and helped them over their grief.

"I don't know what I would have done without him. I really needed him and he was there to help. I really appreciated his help when I needed it the most."

There is a saying that when people need them, God sends angels. John was Mary's angel. God also sent Mary's aunt from Virginia to help her sort through the financial issues of her mother's estate.

Mary met Joseph after her mother died. Aryk didn't like Mary dating. He had never known her to see a man consistently. He tried to kill Joseph four times, but Joseph continued to come to Mary. He loved her and her children. One time, Aryk threw a brass lamp at Joseph. The police were called. Mary had to go to court at least 13 times. She was told that Aryk needed care around the clock. It broke her heart, but she put Aryk in a residential facility for his behavior.

"I resisted, but friends told me that I wouldn't want him to grow into a man hitting people."

Although she didn't want to do it, the residential

facility was the right move because he is now an upstanding citizen. He is in restaurant management, married and happy in Minnesota. He remains her Sweet Potato, but now that he has a son himself, the grandson is her Little Sweet Potato.

Aryk met a girl in Minnesota online. He regularly communicated with her online. He fell in love with her. Although he was supposed to go to college, he decided to move to Minnesota instead. He ended up marrying her. Lisa's story follows.

Being stubborn started when Lisa was born. She was supposed to be born on her mother's birthday of Aug. 14, but she arrived on Aug. 13.

She grew up on a farm for most of her life, but that didn't diminish her interest in cooking at all. From helping her mom in the kitchen to using whatever she could find in the woods, she played with flavors and foods. She watched every cooking show on television and the computer.

She attended Wca School District until she graduated. At this time, she met Aryk. They met online in a nerdy chat room when they were 12, and they became friends. From friendship and chat rooms, they began to be pen pals, talk on the phone and grow in love. When they both graduated, Aryk visited Minnesota, but he never left.

They dated while Lisa went to college at the University of Minnesota. Lisa decided to change schools for the local tech school for art. However, Lisa never lost her passion for cooking. Aryk teased Lisa about being a starving artist watching cooking shows. Things progressed, and they were married. Then promptly nine months later, their son, Derek was born.

Now, she has a whole new reason to love cooking. It brings her so much pleasure to make food for friends and family to enjoy. People never leave her home hungry, but they are frustrated that Lisa doesn't write down her recipes or use formal measurements. But it doesn't stop her from doing the best she can with what she has or try new things with food.

Although Ryan was easier to raise, Mary still had challenges with him. Since he was two years old, Ryan had severe asthma. When Aryk was in a residential facility and newborn Solomon was learning how to stay alive in All Children's Hospital, Ryan was in the hospital with a life-threatening asthma attack. Ryan had gone in and out of hospitals for his asthma throughout his life. He was born of a father who Mary thought was the right man for her. Everyone else didn't like him. Her marriage to Ryan's father was short-lived because he wouldn't support her or his child.

Despite his physical challenges, Ryan would do as he was told and followed the rules for the most part. When he was an adult, he held jobs here and there before entering the Army. He served for two terms. He was stationed in South Korea and attended cooking school while in the Army. Although Ryan was married at Fort Drum, N.Y., the marriage didn't last long. He was living in Dunedin, Fla., with his parents, but moved. He was attending St. Petersburg College and studied real estate and marketing. He wants to be a commercial real estate agent for high-end projects.

His challenges began to surface after Ryan was an adult. When he was stationed in Korea, the North Koreans blasted the barracks with propaganda via loud speakers. He threatened their lives every night. this propaganda led to Ryan developing post-traumatic stress disorder. Ryan wouldn't sleep. He would carry a knife everywhere and wave it when he felt threatened. He got a pitbull puppy that helped with his PTSD somewhat, but it wasn't enough therapy. His behavior with the knives and lack of sleep scared Mary. His behavior escalated. She thought his paranoia was hitting a peak, which was a danger to himself, Solomon, Joseph, Mary and the pets. She recommended that he be placed in a hospital. At the hospital, Ryan got seven to 11 hours of sleep and was doing much better handling his PTSD. When he left the hospital, he decided to move to Minnesota to be near Aryk and Lisa. Ryan also smokes, which is a danger to his asthma and the people around him. Mary prays for his health, both physically and mentally.

Although they can be a challenge to raise, children are blessings from God. The right foods, constant love and God's help can transform unruly kids into responsible adults. All three of Mary's sons are good people.

(Vegetables: a plant or part of a plant used as food, typically used as accompaniment to meat or fish. Examples are cabbage, potatoes, carrots or beans.)

Classic Mashed Potatoes

Ingredients:

Six large rustic potatoes, peeled and diced large

Eight garlic cloves, peeled and whole

Two tablespoons of salt

Salt and pepper to taste

One stick of unsalted butter, cut into pads

Add potatoes to large pot. Add water to an inch above potato line. Add two tablespoons of salt. Add garlic. Place on burner at medium-high temperature. Bring to a boil at high simmer. Cook potatoes until they become tender. Remove and drain. Add contents back into pot. Add butter, salt, pepper and milk. Take potato masher to mash until potatoes and garlic are soft and creamy. Add to serving bowl. Add pads of butter, salt and pepper to garnish. Add slices of cheese.

Green Bean Casserole

Two 15-ounce cans of green beans, drained

Two cups of French fried onions

Two cans of cream of mushroom soup

Three-quarters of a cup of milk

Salt and pepper to taste

16 ounce of shredded cheddar cheese

In a medium-sized bowl, add the green beans. Add mushroom soup and milk. Stir to combine. Fold in eight ounces of the cheese and onions. Stir until well-combined. Add to oven-safe baking dish. Spread the remaining cheese over top. Place in preheated oven at 375 degrees for 15 to 20 minutes. Make sure the onion and cheese are browned and bubbly. Remove from oven. Enjoy.

Honey-Glazed Carrots

Ingredients:

Two pounds of peeled carrots, cut into large chunks

Three-quarters of a cup of honey

Half a cup of light brown sugar, packed

Salt and pepper to taste

Three-quarters of a stick of softened salted butter

In a large pot, add carrots. Add water to an inch above the line of carrots. Add butter, salt, pepper, honey and brown sugar. Put on burner. Set to medium-high. Start boiling. Turn down to medium. Cook until water is almost evaporated. Pour honey caramel sauce over carrots. It is very good.

Jiffy Corn Casserole

Ingredients:

Eight ounces Jiffy corn muffin mix

15-ounce can whole kernel corn drained

15-ounce of creamed corn, not drain

One cup of sour cream

Two tablespoons of sugar

Three lightly beaten eggs

One teaspoon of vanilla extract

Half a cup of melted butter

One eight-ounce package of shredded cheddar cheese

In a large bowl, add melted butter, cornbread mix, eggs and sugar. Whisk to combine. Add creamed corn. Add whole kernel corn followed by sour cream. And vanilla extract. Mix all ingredients well. Add to a 9 x 13 baking dish. Add cheese on top. Bake in a 375-degree preheated oven until toothpick inserted in center comes out clean. Remove and serve. Delicious. (*I like to serve this on the side with chili and rice.*)

Lima Beans

Ingredients:

Two pounds of frozen lima beans

One yellow onion, cut fine

One pound of ground sausage

Quarter cup of salted softened butter

Salt and pepper to taste

Two cups of chicken broth

In a large deep-sided saute pan, brown sausage. Make sure to break up and drain juices. Place back on stove, adjusting temperature to medium high. Add onion, salt and pepper. Cook until onions start to sweat. Add lima beans, cooking for five minutes. Stir constantly. Add chicken broth. Add butter and lid. Cook on low until chicken broth is almost gone and it starts to thicken. Remove from heat and enjoy.

Louise's Zucchini and Eggs

Ingredients:

One large zucchini

Three eggs

One onion, sliced

Salt and pepper to taste

One teaspoon oregano

One teaspoon dried parsley

One tablespoon Parmesan cheese

One tablespoon of olive oil

Pour olive oil in skillet. Heat on medium heat. Add onion. Cook until tender. Cut zucchini into medium slices. Put into pan. Brown on both sides. Add seasonings, except cheese. Beat eggs. Add to pan. Use spatula to move eggs from sides to center. Capture zucchini in eggs. Cook about five minutes. When zucchini is tender and eggs are cooked, add cheese. Cook for another two minutes. Move to plate. Serve from plate.

Mom's Candied Sweet Potatoes

Ingredients:

Six large sweet potatoes, peeled and diced large

Three-quarters of a cup of melted salted butter

Three-quarters of a cup of packed brown sugar

One teaspoon of cinnamon

Mini marshmallows

Boil sweet potatoes until they are fork-tender. Drain. Set aside.

In a small saute pan, add butter. Add brown sugar and cinnamon. Cook on medium-low for about five minutes until bubbly. Remove from stove. Add potatoes to a buttered baking dish. Add brown sugar and cinnamon over potatoes.

Put in a 375-degree preheated oven. Bake until brown and bubbly. Remove from oven. Sprinkle desired amount of mini marshmallows over top. Place into broiler until marshmallows are brown. Remove from oven and serve.

Mom's Green Beans

Ingredients:

Three bags of frozen green beans or three pounds of fresh green beans, cleaned

Three strips of bacon

Half a cup of salted butter

Salt and pepper to taste

Half of an onion, chopped

In a large pot, melt butter. Add onion, salt and pepper. Saute onions until they begin to sweat. Add green beans. Add water until the water covers the green beans. Add raw bacon. Bring to a boil. Move pot to back burner. Set on medium heat. Cook for one and 1/2 hours. Most of the water will evaporate once beans are tender. Place in serving bowl. They are ready to eat.

Peas and Mushrooms

Ingredients:

One pound of medium-sized button mushrooms

Half a cup of salted butter

Salt and pepper to taste

One tablespoon of Worcestershire sauce

Two cups of small frozen sweet peas

Add butter to medium-size sauce pan at medium heat. Once butter is melted and sizzly, add mushrooms. Cook until mushrooms are welded down. Add salt and pepper. Add Worcestershire sauce. Stir. Add peas. Once peas are thoroughly heated, add to serving dish. Garnish with pads of butter.

Rebecca's *au Gratin* Potatoes

(*This is a good way to use up leftover cheese.*)

Ingredients:

Six rustic potatoes, peeled and sliced thin

One sweet onion, peeled and diced fine

Quarter cup of flour

Salt and pepper to taste

16 ounces of shredded cheese, any flavor

Half-and-half

In a large baking dish, add half the slice potatoes, salt, pepper and half of the butter. Cut butter into pads. Spread over potatoes. Add onion. Add half the cheese, followed by the rest of the potatoes, salt and pepper. Add remaining cheese. Pour half and half to the baking dish halfway. Place in preheated 375-degree oven for an hour and a half until potatoes are fork-tender. If cheese is getting too brown, tent with aluminum foil. When done, remove from oven and enjoy. (*As a side note, you can add a pound of ground beef, drained; ham; or chicken. Add meat between the two layers of potatoes.*)

Roasted Yellow Summer Squash

Ingredients:

Six medium-sized summer squashes

One quarter cup of olive oil

Four cloves of garlic minced

Salt and pepper to taste

One tablespoon of herbs of Provence

Lay squash on cutting board. Cut squash in half lengthwise. Using a spoon, remove seeds. Cut squash sideways into one-inch pieces. In a medium-sized baking pan, lay out squash. Toss squash with salt and pepper, herbs of Provence and oil. Keep squash in one layer. Place in preheated 425-degree oven. Bake for 20 minutes. After half of time has elapsed, take a spatula and turn over to other side. Bake until brown. Remove from oven and serve.

Steamed Broccoli and Cheese Sauce

(Use cheese sauce recipe in the Cheese section.)

Two heads of broccoli cut into flowerettes

A half a cup of melted salted butter

Salt and pepper to taste

One cup of water

In a medium-sized saucepan, add water. Bring to a boil. Gently add broccoli. Let water steam broccoli. Add lid to pot for five minutes. Remove from pot. Place in serving dish. Drizzle with butter, salt and pepper. Cover with cheese sauce to finish.

BEVERAGES

DRINK WITH FRIENDS, SHARE PROBLEMS

The people we meet who share our lives makes life wonderful. Some have similar experiences and can commiserate over a glass of wine. These are the close friends who listen to our problems and support us when there are worries or trouble. Others have lives that inspire us to be the best we can be. These are the people we might meet for a short time, but they make all the difference. When people get together, a punch or mixed drinks are served. Parties also include nonalcoholic drinks for those who prefer not to drink alcohol or for children. During these times of celebration, the talk usually involves special memories. Share a drink with your friends and pay heed to these memories.

Sarah and Mary shared many similarities. They both attended the same high school, but they were in different crowds. They both got a day care license for special needs children. In Florida, day care providers must attend a special class in the Challenges Program. At one point, they lived across the street from each other, but it wasn't time for God to bring these friends together.

When Mary's mother died, it left a hole in her heart. It also left her with a problem. Her mother watched Aryk during the day after school before Mary came home from Bon Appetite. She had to shuffle her boys from day care to day care. No one wanted to deal with Aryk's behavioral issues. Mary was desperate for someone to help her with her child. Mary turned to her supervisor in the Challenges

Program and asked who she recommended. The supervisor told her to call Sarah.

During her break at the restaurant, Mary went to the pay phone at the marina and stood in the cold rain to call Sarah. Sarah told her that she needed to meet with Mary and Aryk to interview them both. She wanted to ensure the day care was a good fit. And, Sarah took mostly young children. However, Mary begged her to take Aryk without the interview because she was a single mother and couldn't take time from work to get her son a place to go. At this point, Aryk was in a special school but needed a place after those hours. Sarah agreed. Mary knew that it was right because Sarah was recommended by her supervisor and it felt right. Aryk did well with Sarah. He fit into her program and helped with the younger kids.

From then until now, Sarah has remained a cherished friend of Mary. They found out they had a lot in common. In addition, Sarah helped Mary when she needed it. Early in their friendship, Sarah took Mary to Countryside Church for a Wednesday night service. People who attended the Wednesday night service could get help from the church to pay their utilities. This was just one time over their 20-year friendship where Sarah helped Mary. Sarah is the type of person who will help anyone. Over the years, they bonded like sisters. They would go to lunch together regularly and discuss their children, families and problems. They also hosted parties for products, such as candles or containers. They celebrated birthdays, weddings and Christmases together.

When Solomon was born and Mary decided to be a stay-at-home mom because he couldn't go into day care, Sarah helped Mary get recertified so Mary could help Sarah in her day care three days a week. Whenever Mary needs someone for extra support, Sarah is there because she understands Mary's feelings. For example, they both lost their mothers when the mothers were young. Now, they celebrate their marriages (more than 37 years for Sarah, 20 for Mary), their children and their grandchildren. Sarah's friendship was a gift from God.

Sarah was doing little things for Mary. For example, Joseph bought tickets to see Paul Rodgers in concert. The tickets were one row behind the meet-and-greet row of people. Joseph could not afford to upgrade the tickets to include the meet-and-greet. Sarah bought Mary a ticket for the meet-and-greet row, but didn't go with her. Therefore, Joseph and Mary were not seated together. Mary got dressed in clothes with a lot of sparkles. When Mary met Paul Rodgers, she had an idea. If he needed a personal chef, she would use the opportunity to try for the job even though she had no idea if he wanted a personal chef. She got a gift bag together. Inside the bag, she had her resume. She talked with Paul Rogers who said to Mary that she was wearing a lot of bling, referring to her sparkly clothes. She thought him nice. She will never forget meeting and talking with Paul Rodgers.

God knows the right time for everything. He has a plan. He puts people together when it is supposed to happen. This is true for Mary and Janet.

Janet became Mary's friend when Mary needed financial advice. Her previous adviser couldn't help her, so Janet's regional vice president asked Janet to take over Mary's portfolio. Janet met with Mary and began talking with her. After a long conversation that had little to do with financial advice, Janet and Mary realized they had much in common. For example, both were on their second marriages. Both had step children who are adults now. Both struggled with reaching one or two children who would rather they not have step parents. Both have a food background. Janet's grandparent had a bakery and her mother owned a restaurant. Janet worked in a restaurant until 1988. Both Janet and Mary use food as a way to show love to the people they nurture.

As a gift to her clients and people in her network, Janet gives journals. She talks about using them for gratitude. While Mary doesn't use a journal to write her dreams or gratitude due to her dyslexia, the journal led to a discussion about her dream of publishing a cookbook. Janet told her she knew someone who could help her. At first, Janet told Mary to contact Suzie, but Suzie was having problems and couldn't start a project like this. Plus, Janet never saw Suzie and Mary as a good fit. In the meantime, Janet told Mary she would keep looking for someone to help her. During that time, Janet held a weekly networking meeting for Christen women business owners. She was testing another chapter in St. Petersburg. Louise walked into the meeting with her daughter. A light bulb had clicked with Janet. She asked Louise if Louise helps authors with books. Louise said she does. Janet gave Louise Mary's name and Mary Louise's name. Janet became a messenger from God connecting the two who would fit together for the cookbook project.

Louise grew up in Drexel Hill, Pa., a suburb southwest of Philadelphia. She is the youngest of four children. Her parents are both still alive. She is close with her siblings, their spouses and her niece and nephews. In addition, her grandmother on her mother's side was one of nine children. Her grandfather on her mother's side was one of 10 children although five died in childhood. Her grandmother on her father's side was one of six children. Her grandfather on her father's side is one of three siblings. The point is that Louise comes from a big extended family on both sides. She grew up knowing and spending time with her first, second and third cousins. At the time, Louise thought this was normal. Her family was considered small in elementary school where the average family had eight or nine children. When she entered high school, college and life after college, she learned that knowing first cousins is rare in itself, but, to know second and third cousins was unique. Food and family were always part of every celebration.

Every summer, her mother's cousins got together for a big Fourth of July party at their pool in Delaware. They also came to the shore for two weeks in July and August. Her father's cousins would come to the shore over the first two weeks in August. Louise's parents had a house in Cape May, N.J., where they spent all summer. Her grandmother lived upstairs until she died. Then, it was rented to tourists. Her great aunt and uncle shared the driveway and lived in a house behind hers. The cousins, aunts, uncles and great aunts and great uncles would get together during these weeks. Louise remembers one night her cousins on her mother's side and her cousins on her father's side were all together at Louise's parent's house. A thunderstorm knocked out the power in the middle of the ice cream-making party. Then, it became a lot of laughter and telling stories of storms.

This extended family turned out many nurses, scientists, real estate developers, contractors, carpenters, construction workers, handymen, financial experts, military personnel and teachers, but it boasts only one writer. Louise never had a doubt that she would become a writer. At age eight, she wrote a song. The local newspaper, *Town Talk*, published her first poem when she was 12. She kept diaries although most of the entries are boring. She created stories with her stuffed animals. She wrote a poem for any family event or issue, such as a friend's mother's death or Louise's loneliness. She wrote poems about loved ones and boyfriends. She wrote poems for children and friends. Most often, she was asked to do it. Her mother hired her to write a brochure for the Cape May house. It featured three apartments and one studio, which were rented. Louise's mother ran it like a bed and breakfast and the brochure reflected that. The first book she edited for someone was from her great uncle. He wanted to pass down his stories to the family.

Before the brochure and book, Louise wrote obituaries for a local paper, delivered newspapers and wrote for her high school paper. She attended the University of Maryland College of Journalism because she wanted to tell people the news they needed to know. After college, she had a number of journalism jobs that shaped her life today. Besides the number of jobs, Louise had to deal with a few challenges during her career. She was unemployed about the same number of times, she had a job. She moved from Philadelphia to Baltimore, from Baltimore to Arizona, from Arizona to Baltimore, and from Baltimore to Florida. Although she had full-time jobs, she started her company when she was unemployed. She kept doing it even when she worked full-time. It evolved as technology has evolved. She started working full-time with her company when she moved across the country the first time. It was easier to do this, but she held part-time jobs in Arizona too.

Her children were both joys and challenges for her and they affected her career choices. At age 3 ½, Louise's middle child started showing signs of behavioral problems. He was put into special education classes for pre-school. The problems got continually worse until he was diagnosed with ADHD, sensory integration dysfunction and oppositional defiance disorder. And, he wasn't the only problem. Her eldest child didn't like school. He would be difficult to get out of bed in time for the bus. He would fall asleep in class. He wouldn't do his homework. He eventually failed his classes and dropped out of high school in Florida. He got into trouble with the law and went to jail. He got his general equivalency diploma while in jail. Her youngest child was gifted and talented and needed special education in a different way. The calls from teachers occurred almost daily beginning in Arizona. The third child had difficulty finding challenging classwork in Florida.

Because of these challenges, Louise used her gift for writing to help soothe her worries and concerns. She wrote poems. She wrote her first novel. She wrote a children's series based on her middle son. And, she used her writing to be available when teachers called and still provide an income to her family. Louise's husband has supported the family through all of this and continues to bring the lion's share of the money into the household, but he wouldn't have been able to respond to the teachers as easily. That is why they work so well together. Her husband always has supported her business and her dreams.

Louise met Mary at a time of great financial stress. She had just lost two clients. Her daughter started college and needed money for a number of things. Her husband's salary was strapped paying for all the bills. She needed a project and a big one. She prayed that God would help ease her burdens and find her some work. At the same time, Mary was being told to pursue her dream of writing a cookbook, but she believed she couldn't do it. She was unsure her cookbook would come to fruition because of her dyslexia. She prayed for guidance. Mary had asked for help to write it from Janet who recommended Suzie first. Suzie was having problems of her own and couldn't help Mary.

Louise attended the Effective Christian Women's Networking meeting with her daughter. She often attended networking events to talk about her business. She knew

Janet from other networking meetings. Janet asked if Louise helped authors write and publish books. Louise assured her she did. She gave Louise Mary's phone number and gave Mary Louise's number. Louise had planned to call her the next day, but Mary called first. They had a long phone conversation. Louise realized that Mary shared her motherly experiences with a troublesome child. They had other things in common, such as both were from Baltimore. They were around the same age. They both had to deal with schools and teachers. They both believed in God's plan. Louise adopted two boys. Mary was adopted. Louise understood disabilities. Coming from a large family, Louise understood why food goes with family celebrations or turmoil. Mary decided to take a chance and hired Louise to help her with the cookbook. God knew that Louise was the right person to write Mary's cookbook. He also knew that Louise would help Mary spiritually because Mary suffers from self-doubts, but Louise constantly reminds Mary that everyone has gifts. We are all part of His body. Hers is food. Louise's is writing. He put them together at the right time to get this project going. Now, Mary is excited because she sees that her book will be completed.

(Drink: a liquid intended for human consumption. Besides its basic function of satisfying thirst, drinks play important roles in human culture. Common drinks include plain water, milk, coffee, tea, hot chocolate, juice and soft drinks.)

Coffee

Ingredients:

Coffee grounds, *espresso* beans or Keurig cups

Sugar in the raw

Honey

Creamers

Chocolate drink powder (optional)

Whipped cream (optional)

Butterscotch topping (optional)

Chocolate fudge (optional)

Caramel topping (optional)

Peppermint candy (optional)

To make an iced Keurig bar, buy assorted Kuerig cups for tea and coffee. It's also good to have chocolate drink powder, whipped cream. Butterscotch topping, chocolate fudge, caramel and even a few chocolate sprinkles. (*Make the coffee your own. Have fun. Guests can create whatever they desire.*)

Drinking Water

Ingredients:

Water

Ginger mint

Lemon wedges

Ginger mint

Herbs

Fresh fruit

It's a very good idea to have good drinking water on hand. (*I always keep gallons of purified drinking water in my pantry.*) Take water from refrigerator and drink by themselves or pour over ice with lemons. Using bottles of drinking water, pour into a pitcher diffuser, a pitcher with a tube in the center. Add fruit, herbs and mint to create flavored water.

Festive Punch

Ingredients:

One two liter bottle of ice-cold ginger ale

Half a gallon of ice-cold Hawaiian Punch fruity red

Half a gallon of rainbow sherbet

Add ginger ale and punch to bowl. Add sherbet to the top.

Let it float.

Hot Chocolate

Ingredients:

One cup of whole milk

Three tablespoons of chocolate milk powder or malted milk powder or tablespoon and a half of each to make a malted hot chocolate

Whipped cream

Mix all ingredients into a small saucepan. Heat on high until milk is scalded. Be careful not to break milk. Remove from heat. Add whipped cream on top.

Ice Cream Drinks

Ingredients:

Vanilla ice cream

Flavored sodas

Add scoops of vanilla ice cream to sodas. Grape soda and vanilla ice cream is called a Purple Cow. Orange soda and vanilla ice cream is a Creamsicle. Root Beer Floats uses root beer and ice cream. Try Cola and ice cream also. However, ice cream doesn't work well with ginger ale.

Iced Tea

Ingredients:

Water

Tea bags

Fruit

Herbs

Ginger mint

In a two-quart pitcher that has a tube, called a pitcher diffuser. pour in water. Add tea bags. In the center, add fresh fruits, fresh herbs and mint. Get flavored tea.

Lemonade

Ingredients:

Three and 1/2 cups of water

Half a cup of sugar

Three lemons

In a saucepan, add half a cup of water and sugar. Bring to a boil. Remove from heat. Let cool for 10 minutes. Remove skin from lemons. Create lemon zest. Add zest to the liquid. Let steep for about a half hour. Take a pitcher. Add three cups of water. Squeeze juice from rest of the lemons. Strain syrup from lemon zest. Add to pitcher. Stir well. Add ice and serve. (*It's also nice to add a fresh mint as a garnish.*)

Louise's Red Wine Toddy

Ingredients:

Half cup sugar

One bottle of burgundy or other dry red wine

Two cloves

One teaspoon grated lemon rind

One cinnamon stick

Half cup of brandy

Lemon wedges

Place sugar in a saucepan. Pour wine into pan. Stir until sugar dissolves. Add cloves, lemon rind and cinnamon stick. Heat almost to boiling. Turn off heat. Pour in brandy and mix well. Place lemon wedge in glass. Wrap napkin around each glass before pouring in wine. (*I have made this for Christmas parties. My guests have loved it.*)

Mom's Delicious Eggnog

Ingredients:

Three whole raw eggs or whole raw pasteurized eggs

Two cups of whole milk

Two tablespoons of sugar

A dash of salt

One teaspoon of vanilla extract

A pinch of cinnamon

Place all ingredients in a blender. Mix until frothy. If you wanted to make a spiked eggnog, add a couple shots of dark rum.

DESSERTS

VACATIONS ADD FUN, SWEETNESS TO OUR LIVES

Most people can talk about a vacation where many things went wrong. Several comedy movies have focused on that theme. Still, vacations are necessary to life. They give families a chance to come together and solve problems together. They give families a chance to see and experience new things. Families get a chance to recharge the batteries from hectic lives and routines of home. Vacations are fun and relaxing the same way desserts are fun and relaxing. Ice cream parties can bring people together like a good vacation. People often will have cookie-baking marathons. These social moments are fun and sweet and bring families together. Churches also celebrate with desserts. They will have bake sales or buy a cake when parishioners have done something extraordinary. They sell chances for vacations at these dessert events. When things happen on a vacation, remember to celebrate the positives. So, take a vacation and have some desserts.

At the end of 2018, Mary had the opportunity to connect with Joseph's grandchildren and Anna. They had planned to travel for three weeks out West. It has been Mary's dream to see the country and to see John Denver's sanctuary and the Stanley Hotel, but mostly, Mary wanted to spend time with the children and grandchildren. Solomon came on the trip and celebrated his 18th birthday during the trip. Before the trip, Anna asked Mary and Joseph to buy gift cards to restaurants and to make reservations for any things they wanted to see. They would have to come up funds for the airfare and other purchases. Anna would cover the hotel and rental van. This way, everything would be prepaid and provide fewer worries for the family as they traveled West. Joseph had to borrow money from his boss to cover the gift card purchases.

Before they left, Mary had a Christmas dinner on Dec. 17. They left the next day and arrived in Las Vegas for stop No. 1. Mary wanted this vacation to last as long as possible because it was a once-in-a-lifetime trip. They stayed at the New York, New York casino. Joseph and Mary took romantic walks along the strip while the others took in shows, such as magic, animals and Siegfried and Roy. They also rode a roller coaster. They took pictures at landmarks and enjoyed themselves. While staying in Vegas, they took a day trip to the Hoover Dam.

Next on the itinerary was the Grand Canyon. However, the Grand Canyon Plaza Hotel was two and half hours from the Skywalk. When Mary walked on the Skywalk, she thought she floated in the air. She also enjoyed visiting an Indian reservation. Colorado came next. They saw John Denver's sanctuary in Aspen, Colo. John Denver's music comforted Mary in her youth during those long nights her mother was in Maryland. The family also visited the Stanley Hotel. While in Colorado, Anna had locked the keys in the ignition. A locksmith was called to open the van. After that problem was resolved, they went skiing in Aspen. The grandchildren had never seen snow because they were born and raised in Florida. This was a special moment for Mary and Joseph to watch them enjoy the snow and what Colorado had to offer. Mary and Joseph were given a horse and carriage ride in Denver, which was one of the highlights of the Colorado portion of the trip. However, despite the good times, tensions were beginning to mount.   The group arrived in Salt Lake City for Christmas Eve. They had a nice dinner at Outback. The plan was to leave early Christmas Day to arrive in San Jose, Calif., before the end of the day. But "the best laid plans oft go awry." Anna did not know how to drive in snow and ice. The van skidded on black ice. Anna didn't know what to do and slammed on the brakes hard. This caused the van to spin and pop a tire. It ended up in a salt flats ditch. However, no one was hurt. That was a Christmas miracle. The Utah state police came to assess the damage and to clear the accident, but tow trucks did not want to come get the van from the ditch on Christmas Day. Eventually, the family convinced one, but he was expensive. The tow truck driver helped Joseph to put on the spare tire. After getting the spare tire put on the rim and the van towed, Anna didn't want to drive any more. Joseph took over the driving. The family drove to Reno, Nev., and stayed in a hotel at a truck stop that turned out to be a casino. When they finally got to San Jose, it was very late. The next day, Mary, Joseph and Solomon had tickets to Winchester House. Anna and the grandchildren decided to stay in the van and rest. Because they were going to be in the van, Mary decided to leave her purse in the van with the others. Mary was self-concious about people's feelings regarding theft.

But, Anna decided to leave the parking lot of the Winchester House where there were security personnel and go to a mall in an unsafe neighborhood filled with gangs. She didn't know where the mall was or what the area was like. After shopping at Burlington Coat Factory for shoes for the grandchildren, the shoppers saw the van was robbed. A glass window was smashed. Mary's purse and much of the luggage was stolen. Mary and Anna lost their drivers' licenses. All the gift cards Joseph bought were in Mary's purse, which were stolen. Mary also lost her medicine bag. The police said it could have been worse. The gangs could have kidnapped the grandchildren or Anna. This was the second Christmas miracle. No one was kidnapped; only packages and money were taken. After this happened, Mary wondered why they spent all the money to buy the gift cards. However, this had caused a lot more friction among the family members. Joseph paid for the window to be replaced.

In Santa Cruz, Calif., Mary couldn't enjoy the boardwalk. She was upset over what happened, but they visited the Disney museum and replaced the tire in San Francisco. While in San Francisco, the family saw the house that was used for the exterior of the *Full House* house. Anna decided she wanted to fly back to Florida and end the vacation. Mary and Joseph were willing to go back too. However, to fly, Mary and Anna needed to replace their identifications. Anna called Florida Department of Transportation and filled out the request online to get a new license but didn't bother to do this for Mary. The next day, Anna decided to stay and finish the vacation.

Before the trip, Mary found her biological sister in Fresno, Calif. Therefore, the family added a trip to Fresno so Mary could see her sister. This reunion turned into a disaster. After they went to get pizza, the sister asked if she could spend more time with Mary. Unfortunately, they had prepaid reservations to Disneyland the next day. The sister got angry that they thought Disneyland was more important than her. Joseph pointed out that no one knew about her when the tripped was planned and added a separate trip for the reunion. This was not good enough. Mary didn't enjoy this and left her sister wishing she hadn't done this.

Finally, they reached Disneyland. They had reservations at Paradise Pier. Anna was afraid they wouldn't honor the reservations because the license was lost. Crying and telling the whole story made the hotel to be sympathetic. They offered special amenities. They saw the place where Marilyn Monroe and Walt Disney were buried. At Disneyland, the family spent all day and all night there for several nights. The members were not taking care of themselves, which led to the younger grandchild getting sick. The grandchild was vomiting and had a cold on the day they all were supposed to go to Universal Studios for Solomon's birthday. Anna said she had to take the child to the urgent care. Joseph offered to drive both of them to the urgent care but was refused. The other grandchild didn't want to miss Universal. Anna insisted that they take the van to Universal. When the family got back to the hotel at 5 p.m., they went to Olive Garden for dinner. It was meant to celebrate Solomon's birthday. Anna had called family members in Florida saying that Mary and Joseph didn't care about their grandchild, forcing them to walk to the urgent care. To this day, even though Mary set the record straight, the other family members think Mary and Joseph didn't care and took the wrong action. At this point, the family tensions were hitting their peaks. They did see the San Diego zoo, the Hollywood sign, the place of the Manson murders, Santa Monica pier and Malibu before leaving for home.

The plan was to drive to Atlanta and fly from there, but Mary and Joseph didn't want to drive across the country. They explained the situation at the airport and were cleared to fly by Homeland Security. Once in Florida, Mary got a new license.

During the trip, Mary saw homeless families sitting on the steps of a few of the hotels where they stayed. She prayed for them. She thought the trip was good despite the problems. Miracles happened. No one was hurt. They had everything they needed when they needed it. Although the family tensions remain, they all had a good time and came together to experience new things.

(Desserts: Something sweet to end the meal.)

Apple Crisp

Ingredients:

Three pounds of cooking apples, peeled and sliced

3/4 a cup of light brown sugar, packed

One teaspoon of cinnamon

One cup of salted butter, cut up into cubes

One and 1/2 cups of all-purpose flour

One teaspoon of salt

A half a cup of chopped pecans (optional)

One cup of shredded cheddar cheese

In a 9 x 13 baking dish, arrange apples evenly across bottom. Sprinkle brown sugar over top evenly. Sprinkle cheese over top. In a medium-sized bowl, add sugar, salt, cinnamon and flour. Combine ingredients. Add butter. Mix with a pastry blender until it appears to come out as coarse crumbs but not fine. Add pecans. Pour ingredients over the cheese mixture. Place in preheated oven at 350 degrees for 30 to 35 minutes until it appears to be brown and bubbly. Remove from oven and serve.

Aunt Ruth's Bacon Candy

Ingredients:

Two pounds thick cut bacon

One cup brown sugar

½ tsp cayenne pepper

Mix together. Place on grate. Cook for 30 minutes.

Banana Pudding

Ingredients:

Three and 1/4 cups of whole milk

One and 1/4 cups of sugar

Half a cup of all-purpose flour

Half a teaspoon of salt

One teaspoon of vanilla extract

Four eggs beaten

Four egg whites

One quarter teaspoon of cream of tartar

Four bananas, peeled and sliced

One box of vanilla wafers

In a medium-sized saucepan, combine milk, eggs, one cup of sugar, flour and salt. Mix well. Bring to boil over low heat. Stir constantly. Continue to mix and cook for two more minutes. Remove from heat. In a serving dish, add one layer of pudding, followed by one layer of sliced bananas, followed by one layer of cookies laid flat. Repeat layering. In a medium-sized bowl, whip with a mixer egg whites and cream of tartar. After forming soft peaks, add a quarter cup of sugar. Continue to whip until firm peaks form. Add mixture to top of pudding, spreading evenly. Form valleys and more peaks. Place in a 350-degree preheated oven for about five to 10 minutes watching until becomes a golden brown. Remove from oven. Let cool and enjoy.

Carrot Cake

Ingredients:

Two cups granulated sugar

One and a half cups of vegetable oil

Four eggs

Two cups of cake flour

Two teaspoons of baking soda

One and a half teaspoons of salt

Two and a half teaspoons of cinnamon

Three and 3/4 cups of raw shredded carrots

Three-quarters of a cup of chopped walnuts or pecans

Small can of drained crushed pineapple

Preheat oven to 350 degrees. In a medium-sized mixing bowl, mix sugar, vegetable oil and eggs. In another medium-sized mixing bowl, sift together the dry ingredients. Slowly, mix in the dry ingredients into the wet. Fold in pineapple, carrots and chopped nuts until mixed well. Take three 9 inch cake pans. Lay parchment paper into bottoms but not the sides. Line sides of pans and parchment paper with vegetable shortening. Divide batter evenly into all three pans. Place into oven for about 50 to 70 minutes until toothpick when inserted in center comes out clean. Remove from oven. Place on baking racks to cool completely. (*As a side note, my mom used to put it into a well-greased bundt pan. She would slice it. We would have it for breakfast without frosting.*) Flip over each pan, letting the cakes come out when totally cooled. Mix frosting.

Ingredients for Frosting

One and half pounds of powdered sugar

12 ounces of cream cheese, softened at room temperature

One teaspoon of vanilla extract

Half stick of salted butter, softened

In a large mixing bowl, add cream cheese and butter. Using a hand mixer, whip it until smooth. Continue to whip, adding sugar gradually. Add vanilla. Whip until nice and fluffy. Put one of the cakes onto a cake stand or plate. Frost the first cake. Place second cake on top. Frost that. Repeat the same process with the third cake. Frost sides evenly, covering entire cake. Delicious.

Chocolate Cream Pie

(*See recipe for Mom's Coconut Cream Pie.*)

Ingredients:

Two ounces of melted unsweetened chocolate

¾ cup of Heath chips (optional)

¾ cup of Peanut Butter chips (optional)

¾ cup of Butterscotch chips (optional)

When the custard is at the thickened state, add chocolate. Add Heath chips for a chocolate Heath pie garnishing with chocolate heath bars on top. Add peanut butter chips to make a peanut butter pie. Add butterscotch chips to make it a butterscotch pie.

Ice Cream Shops Chocolate Fudge Cake

Ingredients:

Two chocolate cake mixes

Two half gallons of vanilla ice cream, softened enough to spread

Three cups of sugar

Three cups of heavy cream

Three cups of dark cocoa powder

Three sticks of softened salted butter

One can of aerosol whipped cream

One jar of Maraschino cherries

Start by mixing cake mixes, using only one at a time. Take two half sheet baking pans. Add parchment paper to both. Spread Crisco shortening over parchment paper and sides of pans. Use only one pan. Add cake mix batter in pan. Insert pan into 350-degree preheated oven until a toothpick inserted in center comes out clean. Do the same with the next batter and pan. Once both are baked, remove from oven and let cool completely. Place both cakes and pans in freezer until both are completely firm. Remove from freezer. Spread ice cream quickly over top of one cake. Place other cake on top of ice cream. Place back into freezer overnight. Remove from freezer. Cut into serving slices. Wrap each slice with parchment paper, moving quickly enough so ice cream doesn't melt. Keep in freezer. Take a large saucepan. Add melted butter, followed by sugar and cocoa powder. Add milk. Whisk until contents are combined and thickened. Let ingredients cool. Place into airtight container and refrigerate. When you're ready to serve the cake, take out as many slices as you need. Add to serving plates. Remove sauce from refrigerator. Add as much as you need into saucepan to loosen. When it's warm, pour over individual slices of cake. Add whipped cream and a cherry. (*If you want, you could make it with yellow cake and other flavor ice cream. Mix the recipe any way you desire.*)

Louise's *Pasteria* (Italian Rice Pudding for Easter)

(*This recipe has been passed down from my great-grandmother.*)

Ingredients:

One coffee cup of rice, cooked and drained

One and half cups of sugar

Four eggs

Two teaspoons of cinnamon

One tablespoon of vanilla

Two cups of milk

One pound ricotta cheese

Pie crust for 13 by 9 pan

Preheat oven to 350 degrees. In a mixing bowl, mix together hot rice, sugar, eggs and cinnamon. Make sure sugar melts. In another bowl, mix vanilla, milk and ricotta. Add to egg mixture. Blend until smooth and well-blended. Pour into lined 13 by 9 dish. Bake for 15 minutes. Lower oven temperature to 300 degrees. Bake another two hours. Pudding is done when brown on top and bounces back to touch. Serve on Easter morning.

Louise's *Pasteria* for Alex

(*This is a no-sugar version.*)

Ingredients:

Four eggs

1/4 cup of honey

1/4 cup of stevia

One pound ricotta cheese

Pie crust for 13 by 9 pan

Two cups of milk

One tablespoon of vanilla

Two teaspoons of cinnamon

Follow steps for previous recipe. Substitute stevia and honey for sugar.

Marble Cheesecake

Ingredients:

One cup of graham cracker crumbs

Three eight-ounce packages of cream cheese, softened at room temperature

One cup of white sugar

One cup of sour cream at room temperature

One cup of whipping cream at room temperature

Three tablespoons of flour

One tablespoon of vanilla extract

Three eggs at room temperature

Three-quarters of a cup of semi-sweet chocolate

Preheat oven to 350 degrees. Use a nine-inch springform pan. Butter inside and bottom of pan very well. Dust the sides and bottom of pan with graham cracker crumbs. In a large mixing bowl, beat cream cheese and sugar together until smooth. Add sour cream and heavy cream. Beat again until smooth. Add flour and vanilla. Continue to beat until smooth. Add eggs one at a time, beating again after each one until smooth. In a small mixing bowl, add chocolate chips. Put in microwave for 20 second intervals, taking out, stirring and replacing until all chocolate chips are melted and smooth. Remove from microwave. Add one cup of the cheesecake batter into the chocolate mix. Use a whisk to mix until smooth. Pour the rest of the cheesecake batter on top of the graham cracker crust. Add chocolate batter. Make lines and swirls with a knife. Place pan in oven for 60 to 70 minutes until center is set. Remove from oven and let cool completely. Put in refrigerator and let cool overnight. Remove from fridge and take away springform pan from around cake. Slice and serve.

Mom's Coconut Cream Pie

Ingredients:

One 9-inch pie crust

One and half cups of sweetened, flaked coconut

Three and ¼ cups whole milk

Four eggs beaten

Four egg whites

Cup and quarter of white sugar

Half cup of flour

Half teaspoon of salt

One teaspoon of vanilla extract

Quarter teaspoon of cream of tartar

Dry beans

Preheat oven to 350. Put crust into 9-inch pan. Lay

parchment paper over crust. Add dry beans on top of parchment paper. Place in oven until pie crust is golden brown. Remove from oven and let completely cool. Discard parchment paper and beans. In a medium-sized saucepan, combine milk, eggs, a cup of sugar, flour and salt. Mix well. Bring to boil over low heat. Stir constantly. Continue to cook and stir for two more minutes. Remove from heat. Take 3/4 of a cup of coconut and stir into the pudding. Add vanilla and stir more. Add contents into pie shell. Set aside and let cool to room temperature. Add egg whites to a medium mixing bowl. Add cream of tartar. With a hand mixer, start mixing it low. Set on high. Continue whipping egg whites until you start to see soft peaks. Slowly add 1/4 cup of sugar. Continue until you start forming firm peaks. Add to top of custard. With a spatula, form bigger peaks from the meringue. Add the rest of coconut on top of pie. Add to 350 degree oven for approximately five to 10 minutes watching carefully for meringue and coconut flakes to turn slightly brown. Once slightly browned, remove from oven. Put on baking rack on counter to cool. Once cooled enough, put in refrigerator to chill.

Oatmeal Cookies

Ingredients:

Two cups of packed light brown sugar

Two sticks of salted butter, softened

One teaspoon of vanilla extract

Two eggs

One and 1/2 cups of all-purpose flour

One teaspoon of salt

One teaspoon of baking soda

Three cups of old fashioned oats

One cup of chopped black walnuts

Half a cup of raisins

One teaspoon of cinnamon

Quarter teaspoon of nutmeg

Preheat oven to 350. In a mixing bowl, add brown sugar, cinnamon, nutmeg and butter. Mix until fully whipped. Add vanilla. Continue to whip. Add in one egg at a time and keep mixing. In a medium-sized bowl, add flour, salt and baking soda. Slowly add dry ingredients to wet mixture until fully blended. Slowly add oats, pecans and raisins. Take a half baking sheet and line with parchment paper. Add tablespoons of the mixture two inches apart onto parchment paper. (*I usually get 12 cookies per baking sheet.*) Add to oven for about 10 to 15 minutes or until cookies are golden brown. Remove from oven. Let rest for a minute or two. Remove with spatula and put on baking racks or on a

platter. Enjoy.

Penny's Peach Cobbler

Ingredients:

Yellow cake mix or yellow cake made from scratch

Two cans of peaches, drained
Three-quarters of a cup of light brown sugar, packed

One and a half sticks of softened salted butter

Cool Whip

Make the cake mix. In a 9 by 13 pan, add butter. Put in a preheated 350-degree oven. Once butter is melted completely in pan, swirl butter around sides and bottom of pan. Add sugar to bottom of pan. Add peaches on top of sugar, followed by mixed cake batter. Bake in oven for about 30 to 35 minutes or until toothpick inserted in center comes out clean. Remove from oven. Loosen the sides of the cake from the pan with a knife. Invert pan, being careful, onto appropriate-sized cake platter. Serve with Cool Whip on each slice.

Rebecca's Frosted Brownies

Ingredients:

Two packages of chocolate fudge brownie mix

Eight ounces of chocolate, chopped

Half a cup of salted butter, cubed

One and 1/3 cups of whole milk

Two cups of of sugar

One teaspoon of vanilla extract

Water

In a medium-sized saucepan, fill it halfway with water. Take a medium-sized metal bowl and sit it into the saucepan of barely simmering water. Add butter and chocolate into top metal bowl. Whisk until melted. In a blender, add milk, sugar and vanilla. Blend until sugar starts to melt and everything gets incorporated well. Remove metal bowl of chocolate from heat. Pour into blender. Blend until desired thickness. Remove from blender. Spread over top of brownies.

PANDEMIC INSPIRED

EMPTY STORE SHELVES INVITE CREATIVITY IN COOKING

At the writing of this cookbook, the world was dealing with a pandemic of the coronavirus disease. As a result of government lockdowns and curfews, people had few chances to get to the stores. When people did venture out to go grocery shopping, they found many store shelves empty. In the 1940s, the war caused many shortages and rationing. During those years, families had to cook with what they grew in back yards and what they had on hand at the time. Now, this disease and shortages are causing a similar phenomenon to occur. It reminds people that they should keep many products in their pantries because they never know when they will need them. But, because of the shortages, many people had to cook with what they had available. The recipes in this section show what can be done with a little creativity.

The crisis has affected Mary's sons. Aryk is a restaurant manager and has been unemployed. He was able to get help from the government, but he still is struggling. Ryan was going to school and getting paid by the Army to go to college. However, when he left Florida, he stopped taking classes and was stopped getting money. He had a PTSD episode. He threatened his brother and his family. Ryan has since calmed himself somewhat. Solomon had been going through issues of his own. He has had a lot of anxiety, thinking he was going to die. He also didn't believe in God even though he had been to church and has always heard the word of God, but he was unsure. He and his friends created a trance using mushrooms. In this trance, Solomon had a lot of questions and no answers. This increased his anxiety that he was going to die. He wanted to know what happened when he died. Due to his overwhelming anxiety, Solomon was sent to the psychiatric ward of the hospital. While he was in the hospital, one of his friends overdosed, but he was revived. He told Solomon that he saw his grandmother and heaven. He said, "I'm not ready to die, but when I do, I know it will be OK." He came home from the hospital. And, since that episode, Solomon's fears of dying were gone. God reassured Solomon through his friend's experience. He has no heaviness in his heart or other fears.

Beef Skillet

Ingredients:

One pound of beef sirloin steak, cut into strips

One onion, chopped

Six garlic cloves, minced

Four cups of diced potatoes

One quart of beef broth

Two tablespoons of Worcestershire sauce

Two tablespoons of cornstarch

Salt and pepper to taste

One Teaspoon of basil

One teaspoon of oregano

One teaspoon of thyme

Olive oil to brown meat

Six tablespoons of salted butter, cut into six pads

In a large skillet, add olive oil. Turn heat up until sizzling. Add meat. Brown. Add onion. Cook onion until it gets translucid. Add garlic, salt and pepper. Saute for about five minutes. Add in potatoes. Saute for another five minutes. In a bowl, add beef broth. Whisk in cornstarch. Slowly stir mixture into skillet. Add in Worcestershire and seasonings. Stir and lay pads of butter on top of mixture. Cover with foil. Place in preheated oven at 375-degree for about an hour. Remove from the oven and serve. (*As a side note, add in any leftover vegetables. Be creative and make it your own.)*

Black Beans

Ingredients:

Six pieces of bacon, cooked crisp and saving the fat from the skillet

Four cups of black beans, soaked overnight

One large red onion, chopped

Six cloves of garlic, minced

Two carrots, cleaned and chopped

One red and one green bell pepper, chopped

One tablespoon of cumin

One tablespoon of chili powder

One teaspoon of smoked paprika

One teaspoon of basil

Four cups of chicken broth

Water as needed

Salt and pepper to taste

In a six-quart Dutch oven, add bacon grease, onions, garlic, peppers, carrots, salt and pepper. Cook for about two minutes until ingredients have bloomed. Add drained beans and chopped bacon. Add in chicken broth and enough water to cover ingredients over one inch. Place in preheated 375-degree oven for two and a half to three hours or until ingredients have thickened and the beans are tender.

Remove from oven and serve over prepared rice. (*For a side note you can use turkey bacon, but you're not going to have any grease from cooking it, so you'll have to add oil to make up for it. On another side note, when you're preparing your rice and adding the water to it, you can other different flavors of broth instead of water. You can also add different spices. I like cumin and if I'm adding beef broth, I like to add a quarter cup of ketchup. If I'm using chicken broth I like to add a half a teaspoon of turmeric.*)

Ham Hash

Ingredients:

Two tablespoons of vegetable oil

Four cups of diced ham scraps could be leftovers

Three cups of white diced potatoes or even peeled and diced sweet potatoes

Three carrots, peeled and diced

One large onion, peeled and diced

Salt and pepper to taste

Six cloves of minced garlic

One cup of chicken stock

In a large skillet, add oil. Make it hot. Add onions, salt, pepper and garlic. Cook onions until translucent. Add potatoes and carrots. Turn heat down to medium-low. Cover with lid. Stir every few minutes so it doesn't burn or stick to bottom of pan. Once potatoes and carrots are tender, add ham and chicken stock. Cook until ham is well-heated. Remove and serve. (*It's delicious to add chopped cabbage. You can add leftover vegetables. Be creative and adding whatever you desire.*)

Lasagna

Ingredients:

Quarter cup of vegetable oil

One onion, diced

One pound of ground chuck

Four cups of marinara sauce, either from jar or homemade

Eight cloves of garlic, minced

One teaspoon of basil

One teaspoon of oregano

Two tablespoons of light brown sugar

One can of fire-roasted tomatoes

Two bay leaves

Two large containers of whole milk ricotta cheese

One tablespoon of dried parsley

Half a cup of Parmesan cheese

Four cups of shredded mozzarella cheese

One package of oven-ready pasta sheets or one package of cooked lasagna noodles

Salt and pepper to taste

Four large eggs

Using a large skillet, add oil and onions. Saute until tender. Add ground chuck and thoroughly brown. Drain excess oil. Add marinara sauce, tomatoes, seasonings, six cloves of garlic, brown sugar, salt and pepper. Add bay leaves. Stir ingredients. Cover with lid. Cook on medium-low heat for about 30 minutes, stirring occasionally. In a large mixing bowl, add all by half pound of ricotta cheese, eggs, two cloves of garlic, parsley, salt and pepper. Mix ingredients until combined. Add two cups of mozzarella and all of Parmesan cheese. Mix until combined. In 9 x 13 baking dish, spray with cooking spray. Add one layer of sauce. Add a layer of noodles over it, followed by a layer of cheese mix. Repeat process of layering until three layers are created. Once three layers are created, add remaining sauce on top. Add remaining mozzarella cheese over sauce. With remaining ricotta cheese apply a layer like frosting a cake on top. Place on half sheet pan and place in preheated 375-degree oven for about one hour when it looks hot and bubbly and ricotta cheese is golden brown, remove from oven. Let stand for at least 15 minutes. Serve and enjoy. (*This is a good way to use leftover cheese scraps by shredding them to make up four cups.*)

Louise's Stir Fry Beef Meal

Ingredients:

One pound stir fry beef

One can of green beans

One can of mushrooms

One pound of ricotta cheese

One onion, sliced

Two tablespoons of olive oil

Pasta

In a skillet, pour olive oil. Heat. Add onion and beef. Brown beef. Add green beans and mushrooms. Cook for five minutes. Add ricotta cheese. Cook for 10 minutes. Pour over pasta.

Pinto Beans and Rice

Ingredients:

Four cups of pinto beans, soaked overnight

Quarter cup of vegetable oil

One diced onion

Six garlic cloves, minced

One ham bone

Salt and pepper to taste

Four cups of chicken broth

Water

Half cup of ketchup

Quarter cup of yellow mustard

One tablespoon of ground cumin

One teaspoon of paprika

One tablespoon of chili powder

One teaspoon of basil

One teaspoon of oregano

One teaspoon of thyme

One quarter cup of packed brown sugar

Rice

In a six-quart Dutch oven, add oil. Add enough heat to get it sizzling. Add onion, salt and pepper. Cook until translucent. Add spices and garlic. Cook until garlic can bloom. Add drained beans. Stir mixture. Add chicken broth, brown sugar, ketchup and mustard. Stir ingredients. Add ham bone and enough water to create one inch of liquid over mixture. Place into preheated 375-degree oven. Cook for about two hours. Cook until mixture has thickened and beans are tender. Remove from oven. Remove bone. Separately cook rice. (*I prefer jasmine rice.*) Serve beans over rice. Delicious.

Sally's Pork Chops

Four pork chops about an inch and a quarter thick

Three tablespoons of olive oil

Salt and pepper to taste

Two cans of tomato soup

One can of water

Add olive oil to a hot skillet. Add salt and pepper to pork

chops on both sides. Place in skillet. Brown both sides. In a small bowl, add soup and water. Whisk until creamy. Pour mixture over pork chops. (*If you want to add mushrooms or anything else, do so now*) Add to preheated 350-degree oven for about an hour and a half. Remove from oven and enjoy with your favorite side dish. (*I enjoy it with mashed potatoes. You can also substitute pork chops for chicken breasts.*)

CONCLUSION

MIRACLES DO HAPPEN

The stories in this cookbook show that life throws stumbling blocks in your path periodically. Food, family and God are the three elements that will help you move past those obstacles to find joy. Miracles happen every day. Keep your mind open and heart ready to receive the Lord's message and you will see His purpose for you and your life. Accept the trials because they make you stronger and more faithful. The Lord will take care of you even if you don't think He is doing that or if you don't believe. However, He constantly whispers to you through people and places, family and food, and love and friendship.

Mary didn't always believe in God. Still, she felt protected. When she has looked back over her life, she realizes the times that God had helped her. After Mary's mother died and before Mary met Joseph, Ryan got sick. He needed antibiotics that cost more than she had available being a single mother. If Ryan didn't get the antibiotics, he would be put in the hospital. Mary drove to the pharmacy and sat in her car. She knew that she would have to write a bad check to get the medicine because she had no money. Mary felt strong remorse for planning to cheat the pharmacy, but she loved her son so much that she had to get his medicine. When she got up her nerve, she went into the pharmacy and waited for the medicine to be ready. She was nervous. She thought everyone knew she was about to write a bad check and doing it purposely. However, when she got to the counter, the pharmacy technician said someone had paid for the medicine. Mary doesn't know who paid for her son's medicine. No one knew that she needed to pay for the medicine but Mary and God. Mary knows that God sent an angel for her that day.

Nanette, Sarah's sister, didn't believe in God. She lived her life without prayer. In the early 1980s, she was going to the hospital in Seminole, Fla., to visit her mother who was dying of cancer. While approaching her mother's room, she was met by a tall black nurse who asked her, "Are you Nanette, Patricia's daughter?", which she responded that she was. The nurse told her, "I want you to know that I have prayed with your mother and she has received Jesus as her savior. So just know that she will be with Him in heaven." Then the nurse walked away. Not being a believer at the time, Nanette was more upset that her mother would die than comforted at the thought of heaven. As she sat in the hospital room with her mother who was not conscious enough to have a conversation, Nanette began to think and wonder about the nurse. She left the room to go to find her and didn't see her anywhere. She asked at the nurse's station, and everyone there told Nanette that no one there fit her description -- no nurses, workers or aids. Well, Patricia soon seemed well enough to come home for a while only to die a month later. While she was home, Nanette asked her mother about this tall nurse, and Patricia told her she did remember her voice and prayers. When opening her eyes, she saw golden light glowing around this beautiful nurse. A year after her mother's death, Nanette accepted the truth of God's salvation in Jesus and now is comforted in knowing that her mother is with Him and she will see her again one day.

Louise adopted two boys from Russia because she was having trouble conceiving. Everywhere she went, people told her that as soon as she adopted she would get pregnant. Even her doctor told her that. In 1995, Louise conceived her first baby. She took the pregnancy test and miscarried the next day. She also had a dream that year that she was sitting in the doctor's office, and the doctor came running around the corner. She said, "Louise, did you know you are pregnant?" This dream occurred after she had miscarried. She didn't conceive after that. In 1998, her mother-in-law died, which convinced Louise and her husband to adopt. After a year of filling out paperwork and waiting, Louise and her husband were given information about their boys. They went to Russia to bring her two boys home. In 1999, Louise's parents paid for the family to vacation in Paris for the 2000 year. Louise got pregnant again. After seven weeks, she was in a minor car accident. She wasn't hurt. There was hardly any damage, but she miscarried again. Then, Louise lost track of her charting and went to the doctor for her annual check up. The nurse asked Louise when her last period was. Louise couldn't remember. The nurse took a pregnancy test. As Louise waited, the doctor came down the hall and turned the corner and asked, "Louise, do you know you're pregnant?" This announcement happened exactly like in her dream. She knew it must have been a message from God. The second part of the miracle was that when she found out she was pregnant, it was exactly one year after adopting the boys. Her daughter is now an adult, but she will always be her miracle baby. After the adoption, people asked Louise if she wanted to go back for a girl. She would always answer, "If God wants me to have a girl, I will have it the natural way," which is what happened.

Besides this dream, Louise had another two dreams that informed her of her mother-in-law's illness and death before it happened. Her dreams are always vivid and sometimes, God is talking to her.

Miracles occur in the people we meet and share our lives. God has a plan for all his followers. He won't abandoned us. He will guide His people throughout their lives. Take up your cross and follow Him. Take up your spatula and follow the recipes in this book. Enjoy your life and God's miracles!

Thank you for purchasing this cookbook. I hope you have many fun times around the kitchen or dining room table and enjoy the food. Please take time to write me a review on Amazon.

INDEX

D

Dairy

19, 20, 22, 23, 25, 35, 38, 46, 47, 48, 49, 50, 54, 100, 114, 118, 129, 145, 177. See also cheese; See also drinks

butter

20, 21, 25, 26, 34, 35, 36, 37, 38, 39, 40, 48, 49, 50, 51, 54, 55, 57, 58, 60, 61, 84, 85, 86, 90, 91, 94, 95, 100, 102, 103, 104, 105, 106, 107, 108, 113, 115, 116, 117, 118, 119, 120, 121, 123, 128, 133, 143, 144, 145, 146, 147, 148, 149, 150, 171, 174, 175, 176, 179, 180, 181

cheese

19, 20, 22, 23, 24, 25, 26, 27, 36, 38, 39, 40, 46, 47, 48, 49, 53, 54, 55, 56, 57, 58, 68, 69, 72, 83, 84, 86, 95, 100, 106, 107, 113, 117, 118, 120, 123, 128, 129, 130, 131, 132, 133, 134, 135, 143, 144, 145, 148, 149, 150, 171, 174, 177, 190

blue

86, 129, 130

brie

128, 132

cheddar

19, 46, 47, 48, 49, 53, 54, 72, 95, 100, 130, 131, 135, 144, 145, 171

cream

25, 26, 36, 38, 130, 132, 134, 135, 174, 177

feta

72, 133, 134

Monterey Jack

19, 46, 47, 48, 49, 53, 54, 72, 95, 100, 130, 131, 135, 144, 145, 171

Drinks

E

Eggs

21, 23, 24, 33, 35, 38, 56, 68, 69, 70, 71, 72, 84, 85, 89, 90, 101, 103, 110, 113, 114, 115, 116, 117, 118, 119, 120, 121, 133, 134, 145, 164, 172, 173, 174, 177, 178, 179

F

Fruit

19, 21, 22, 26, 161, 190. See also drinks

apples
128, 171

blueberries
33, 37

coconut
21, 22, 66, 67, 175, 178, 179

cranberries
66, 67, 71

lemon
86, 87, 100, 101, 102, 103, 104, 105, 106, 107, 108, 115, 116, 161, 164

orange
22, 33

peaches
180, 181

pineapple
173, 174

raisins
179, 180

tomato

tomato juice

26, 27

tomatoes

19, 20, 46, 47, 48, 50, 51, 54, 55, 57, 58, 59, 71, 82, 83, 131

G

Grains

20

bread

20, 21, 22, 23, 29, 41, 55, 56, 77, 84, 85, 88, 89, 90, 101, 119, 129, 133, 134, 135

fettuccine noodles

106

macaroni

46, 47, 53, 57, 58, 68, 69, 123

rice

47, 48, 49, 53, 87, 106, 145

rolls

34, 36, 37, 38, 39 40

tortilla chips

19

H

Herbs

25, 117, 161, 163

basil

39, 41, 48, 51, 54, 55, 57, 59, 82, 89, 90, 117, 132, 133

bay leaf

48, 61

48, 51, 52, 54, 56, 57, 59, 82, 89, 90, 117

tumeric
52

M
Meat
19, 19–192, 20, 21, 22, 24, 27

bacon
54, 58, 59, 60, 71, 81, 89, 95, 100, 115, 116, 119, 120, 121, 147, 172

beef
19, 20, 24, 43, 46, 47, 48, 51, 53, 57, 89, 90, 92, 93, 94, 95, 113, 149

chicken
20, 22, 42, 43, 48, 49, 50, 51, 52, 53, 54, 55, 56, 57, 58, 59, 60, 61, 66, 69, 82, 83, 84, 85, 86, 87, 107, 108, 129, 131, 146, 149

filet mignon
20, 81

ground chuck
19, 46, 47, 48, 55, 56, 57, 58, 87, 88, 89, 94

ham
48, 49, 50, 51, 58, 59, 60, 61, 69, 83, 84, 131, 132, 133, 135, 149

hamburger
80

kielbasa
27

meatballs
80, 89

meatloaf
88

pork

S

42, 69, 70, 72

V

Vegetables

19, 23, 25.

beans

47, 48, 49, 58, 59, 68, 70, 71, 87, 119, 120, 143, 144, 146, 147, 160, 178

black
48

green
70, 87, 143, 144, 147

kidney
7, 48, 68, 70, 87

navy
58, 59, 119, 120

broccoli
131, 132, 150

cabbage
50, 51, 67, 143

carrots
48, 49, 50, 51, 52, 56, 57, 58, 59, 61, 67, 86, 87, 91, 92, 94, 95, 131, 143, 144, 173, 174

celery
27, 48, 49, 50, 51, 52, 53, 54, 55, 56, 57, 58, 59, 60, 61, 66, 67, 72, 82, 83, 86

corn
24, 81, 145

creamed

CPSIA information can be obtained
at www.ICGtesting.com
Printed in the USA
BVHW060021200620
581883BV00006B/572

9 781513 662220